The Dog Nobody Loved

The Dog Nobody Loved

Frieda, the dog who proved love changes everything

JON KATZ

EBURY
PRESS

3 5 7 9 10 8 6 4 2

First published in the UK in 2013 by Ebury Press, an imprint of Ebury Publishing
A Random House Group company

First published in the USA as *The Second-Chance Dog* by Ballantine Books, an imprint
of The Random House Publishing Group, a division of Random House, Inc., in 2013

The Random House Group Limited Reg. No. 954009

Addresses for companies within the Random House Group can be found at
www.randomhouse.co.uk

A CIP catalogue record for this book is available from the British Library

The Random House Group Limited supports the Forest Stewardship Council® (FSC®),
the leading international forest-certification organisation. Our books carrying the
FSC label are printed on FSC®-certified paper. FSC is the only forest-certification
scheme supported by the leading environmental organisations, including Greenpeace.
Our paper procurement policy can be found at www.randomhouse.co.uk/environment

Printed and bound by CPI Group (UK) Ltd, Croydon, CR0 4YY

ISBN 9780091957445

To buy books by your favourite authors and register for offers visit
www.randomhouse.co.uk

To Maria and Frieda, two strong spirits
who never gave up on each other, or on me

DISCLAIMER

This book is a work of non-fiction based on the life, experiences and recollections of the author. The names of people, places, dates, sequences or the details of events may have been changed to try to protect the privacy of others.

Contents

The Dog Nobody Loved

Chapter One

The Dog Who Kept Men Away

I heard the barking as soon as I pulled into the gravel driveway of the sprawling old farmhouse on a country road about five miles from my farm.

The noise was coming not from the house but from a barn behind it.

It was the deep-throated, door-rattling roar of the guard dog, and there was something undeniably frightening about it. A dog with a voice like that had to be huge and powerful. I had never heard a roar quite like it. None of my dogs ever barked in such a furious, almost panicked way. It was a bark to be taken seriously, very seriously, and I was reminded of the raptor in *Jurassic Park* busting out of its prison.

I was not looking for trouble from a dog. My life, at this

point, was in upheaval. I was spectacularly disconnected from the world and attempting to stave off a crack-up. I tried to soothe my internal turmoil by focusing on fixing up my collapsing Civil War–era farm and barns, at least three of which were about to topple over into the road. Barns were collapsing and being torn down all over Washington County, New York, where I lived, but I was determined that my four would be saved. This project was horrifically expensive and complicated, but I couldn't bear to see these beautiful old structures disintegrate.

I wanted some old windows to put in one side of my big dairy barn so that the grand old red silo housed inside the barn (an unusual feature) could be seen from outside. No real farmer would consider such an insane thing. But at the time, I was not sane. An HBO film crew had just finished making a movie of my trek upstate, and the very air was suffused with unreality.

So, I had come to this place because I'd been told that the couple restoring this farmhouse had some old windows. A thin, wiry woman with short brown hair, wearing tattered jeans, a paint-splattered shirt, and sandals, came out of the door and approached me. As we stood in the drive, she began urging the dog to calm down. "Sssssh, Frieda, quiet," she said. Her voice was so soft and tentative I knew she didn't really mean it, and the dog surely knew she didn't. She was concerned that I might be frightened, but I can tell when somebody means to change a dog's behavior and when they don't.

"We can't have many people over." She smiled, tilting her head back toward the frenzied roaring and charging coming from the small barn.

There was something melancholy about this woman. She was so quiet and reserved. She shyly explained that she and her husband were living in a small barn while they fixed up the farmhouse close by. "Who is that?" I asked, gesturing toward the barn, whose door was still rattling from the force of the dog inside throwing herself against it.

"That's Frieda," she said, surprising me with a radiant smile.

"Nice to meet you," I said. "I'm Jon."

"I know," she said. "I'm Maria. I have to confess," she continued, "I haven't read any of your books." She was small, frail, almost elfin. But I knew I saw some humor in her eyes, attitude, pride. She was restoring houses with her husband, she said, adding almost under her breath that she was also an artist.

"That's okay, most people haven't. Anyway, I can give you one," I said, reaching into the car. I had brought a paperback with me.

I don't know why I'd brought a copy of that book—it was *The Dogs of Bedlam Farm*—for Maria. She looked at it and laughed, and would soon put it aside.

Maria invited me into the barn, into the small room she was living in while working on the farmhouse. I hesitated.

I'm not afraid of dogs generally, of course, but I know that in certain situations protective dogs will defend their people and territory. And Maria did not seem strong or clear with Frieda. I could see that Frieda had not been trained, as Maria had no commands to which the dog readily responded. She just got more excited when Maria spoke to her. When people really want their dogs to behave differently, they're usually more forceful. I have always believed that people get the dogs they need.

Maria needed a guard dog, it seemed. I thought there must be some fear in her. She explained that Frieda did not like men. Okay, I thought, so she needed a guard dog who did not like men.

But I wasn't sure *I* needed Frieda. She was giving me that unmistakable look of the territorial dog: eyes locked on me, ears back, tail down, body stiff. I had expected to pick up the old windows and leave. But that afternoon, I found myself wanting to talk to Maria. There was something very warm about her. I felt a connection I had not felt in so long I barely recognized it. I wanted to know more, to see what was behind those sad and sweet eyes. My farm is in a remote part of upstate New York, and I had not made many friends there. My wife at the time was living in New Jersey, and our visits to see each other were becoming less frequent. It was sometimes lonely. Actually, it was always lonely.

We walked to the barn, and the roaring got even louder. Maria opened the door ahead of me, and I could see her lean over a large brown-and-black mixed-breed dog and pull her back into the corner. The roaring subsided for a bit, and then resumed from the corner. Frieda wasn't trying to charge me; she just clearly wanted me to go away. She was more anxious than aggressive.

I could see right away that Frieda—a rottweiler-shepherd rescue—was like others I had met: loving and devoted to their humans, but ferociously protective of them. Because I write about dogs, people are sometimes embarrassed when I meet theirs. They suspect I am judging them, and they apologize.

The dog was abused, the dog was abandoned, the dog is sweet and good, just overprotective in some situations.

Maria apologized for Frieda's barking. She had never really trained her, she said, but it didn't seem to me that Maria was too bothered by Frieda's loud vigilance.

Still, I have studied attachment theory for years, written books about it, lived it in my own life. It is a prescient window into the lives of some people, how they are with their dogs, how their dogs are with them. Something powerful connected these two.

I looked around the barn. I could see that Maria and her husband were living an ascetic life. No computer. Few possessions. Nothing new or fancy. A spartan place, almost monastic. Lots of books and magazines. No junk or clutter. Different from my life, filled as it was with rolling chaos.

Maria repeated that she couldn't really have many visitors. And she didn't trust Frieda outside, either, around people or other dogs. "I take her for long walks in the woods," she said, "but it's just us." Maria didn't think Frieda was trainable because of the dog's history, and because she was so wild.

She had adopted Frieda from a local animal shelter, where she had been kept for nearly a year. All the shelter workers knew about Frieda was that she was a healthy female (the shelter had spayed her) who had been captured in the southern Adirondacks after a year-long pursuit by one of their animal control officers.

I have kept away from dogs like Frieda all of my life, and would never have considered adopting one or taking one home. For me, dogs are about people, mixing with them, living among them. I would not want a dog that people were afraid of, that you had to watch every second. And looking at Frieda, whose barking had now morphed into a low, menacing growl, I was definitely wary of her.

But I had seen this type of situation before. Sensitive people (often, but not always, women) empathized with dogs who would be put to sleep if they were not adopted, who desperately needed homes. And I knew there was often something else going on. Perhaps a wish to be protected? A complicated childhood? A desire to withdraw from the world? A need to nurture? All of the above? None of the above?

"What made you adopt her?" I asked. The answer would tell me a lot about this woman, and I almost always ask it of people I meet with big, scary dogs.

"Oh, I just thought she was so cute," she said. I smiled.

I moved a couple of feet inside the barn, and when Frieda roared and growled, I moved back again.

So there it was, the beginning of my fairy tale, the kind of story men my age are not supposed to dream of anymore.

This is the story of an aging and troubled man yearning for love and knowing it will never come, a troubled artist who had given up her art and lost her voice, and a courageous, fiercely loyal wild dog abandoned by a bad man and left to fend for herself in the Adirondack wilderness.

There was me, sixty-one, broke and bewildered, beginning to see that his thirty-five-year marriage was falling apart, living alone on a farm in a poor and remote corner of upstate New York with a bunch of animals.

And there was Maria, a sad, brooding fiber artist in her forties, nearing the end of a twenty-year marriage, seeking to find her lost creative soul.

And finally there was Frieda, a.k.a. "the Helldog," a rottweiler-shepherd mix who had been cruelly abandoned and spent years living in the wild.

And what in the world could possibly bind these three completely disparate and seemingly so utterly different beings? The thing that makes any good fairy tale work: we were looking for love. We were looking to be saved from an empty life. We were seeking that rarest of miracles, a second chance.

Maria and I have talked many times about our first meeting. We both remember how easy it was to talk to each other. We felt comfortable with each other. I had many people in my life and was comfortable with few of them. Maria had few people in her life and was not often at ease with any of them.

I know that many people are uncomfortable around me; I have learned this. I make people nervous because I'm restless, because I often focus in on people like the reporter I was for so long, because, without knowing it, I'm almost viscerally compelled to talk about things most people don't really want to talk about. I don't mean to behave this way, but I know I do. I don't like chitchat. I don't let sleeping dogs lie. I have made very few good friends in my life, for various reasons, and until recently, most of them have simply gone away.

I didn't feel so restless with Maria. If I was crazy or intense, she didn't seem to notice or mind. Apart from worrying that

Frieda would tear me to bits, I didn't sense any discomfort at all.

Our lives in the country offered easy ways to get to know each other. We met again, soon after, by a neighbor's burn pile, where anybody in the neighborhood could bring their scrap to burn. The same friend who'd first told me about Maria had called both of us and told us the burn pile would be going and then told each of us the other was coming. When you brought wood and junk to a burn pile, you had to sit there until the fire had burned down. It was common to arrange for some company, as the process could take hours. I called Maria and told her I was coming and offered to bring hot chocolate. It was nearly freezing. She said she would be there.

Maria and I hauled over our logs and brush, and sat by the fire. I'd brought her some books by writers I loved—Jane Smiley, Annie Proulx, Anita Brookner. She already owned the Smiley and Proulx, took the Brookner.

It was so easy to talk to her.

We talked about everything: books, dogs, art.

"Why aren't you making art?" I asked.

She shrugged. "Nobody would want it," she said. She made quilts from recycled fabrics, and many people in the art world didn't consider that art. I knew what she meant. Lots of people in the publishing world didn't consider dog books literature, either.

I did most of the talking, but she listened, curious, sometimes tilting her head at an odd angle.

I got the sense that she was unhappy with her life.

Mostly, that evening by the fire, we talked about dogs. We were both in long marriages, and had anyone suggested to either of us that we would one day not be in those marriages, we would have fainted dead away. Both of us. I never once thought I would get divorced. I said a million times that no matter what happened, I would never get divorced. Maria often said the same thing.

Dogs do not understand things like marriage and divorce; nor are they interested in the twists and turns of the human psyche. Frieda was very nervous around me that day, as well as protective of Maria. I could see it. The panting, the eyes shifting back and forth, the squirming around, the growling. Even then, on that first day, when I was blind to so much, Frieda seemed to sense something happening. She reminded me of my border collies when they hear a storm approaching, many miles away, before I see any visible sign of it. Their eyes narrow, and they circle, whine, growl, and cannot find a place to alight. That was how Frieda behaved as I talked with Maria.

Given her fury, it was hard to get a really good look at this enormous dog, a menacing creature, wolflike and powerful. But every now and then, she would stop barking and look me up and down—and I saw that she had the sweetest brown eyes. I don't know what Frieda was seeing when she looked at me that first day, but I do know she wanted it out of the house.

Maria and Frieda had connected on a very emotional level, each protecting the other, each feeling safe and grounded with the other. Those are the most powerful kinds of human-dog relationships. Also the most confusing.

I remember thinking this: Nobody ought to try to come between Maria and this dog. It never occurred to me for a second that I would be the one to attempt it.

Frieda, it seemed to me, did not know how to live in the world beyond Maria. She had no idea what her job or purpose was, and nobody had yet appeared who could teach her. How interesting, I thought. Because I was in exactly the same situation: at loose ends and purposeless. Looking back, I see that this was our first connection.

Maria was quiet, a good listener, and I enjoyed talking with her, but she was so reserved at times I wondered if she had trouble speaking. You know some people by what they say, and others by what they don't say.

I asked her about it soon after we met, and she looked at me and her eyes filled with tears, and then I understood that she had a voice but had lost it somehow.

Maria said little about her life, nothing about her family or her marriage, even less about her art. She was from Long Island. She'd been an artist once but was not one now, and when she said that, she couldn't hide the pain and sorrow in her eyes. This was one of the problems in my life. I never missed things like that. And I rarely let them go.

Sometimes, she said, it was the art world that made her uncomfortable. It was too commercial. "I wasn't making anything good." Sometimes, she said, it was because she was too busy working to restore houses—hard, physical work—and she didn't have the time.

I told Maria that I thought Frieda might benefit from some basic grounding training, and I could see she was interested. I remember thinking how small a space that barn was for such a big and unnerving dog.

As I left the burn pile that night, I thanked Maria for the windows she had given me and we shook hands. I said we all ought to get together for dinner sometime. We exchanged telephone numbers. We seemed so very different, but I also thought she would make a great friend. That would be nice, but unlikely. Married men and married women don't often become good friends with each other. I didn't really think I would ever see her again.

Chapter Two

The Dog Nobody Wanted

Frieda had entered Maria's life in the fall of 2003, the same year I bought Bedlam Farm. Her Doberman, Lestat, had died a few years earlier, but that was only part of the reason Maria went to the animal shelter outside Glens Falls, New York. Her sister had recently returned a dog to a shelter because it nearly bit one of her children. This would have caused some people to wonder if they wanted a dog at all, but it made Maria feel selfish. There were millions of dogs who needed homes, she reasoned, and so she should get one.

I am one of those people who go through life without ever seeing a wounded bird or animal. Maria can't stop by the grocery store without spotting one. I can't imagine picking up a wounded rabbit from the roadside and taking it home. Maria would never pass such a creature by. She is a whisperer; I saw that right away. She talks to animals, and they talk back.

The rescue impulse has always fascinated me. It's a powerful prism through which people see—or don't see—the world of animals. Ever since Maria was a child, she's been bringing home stray kittens, crippled birds, mice, rabbits, even wounded squirrels. Maria notices the needy things in the world, and identifies with them. When she was a vet tech, she brought home one-winged seagulls, a blind cat named Music, and a three-legged dog named Pitcher. Maria identifies with the outcast creatures of the world and sees herself in them.

At the time she adopted Frieda, Maria and her husband both felt that their remaining dog, Skunk, an affable ten-year-old border collie, would like some company. It didn't take Maria long to find the dog she wanted. In fact, the dog she wanted had been waiting for her for a long time, sitting in a kennel in a nearby animal shelter.

Country shelters tend to be different from city shelters. Here, the idea of a "no-kill" shelter where taxpayers foot the bill for dogs and cats to live out their lives in crates is not considered a rational prospect or a humane act. People who live in the country know that animals do not inhabit a no-kill world. They know animals to be violent, selfish, and ruthless in their natural worlds.

In the country it is considered cruel and unnatural to put animals in crates for years. In underfunded shelters, dogs find homes or they are euthanized. People like to say that some dogs and humans were meant to find one another. That seems to have been the case with Maria and Frieda.

Maria got Frieda the way so many Americans get dogs

these days. "I wanted to do some good, but I didn't really like people at the time," she told me. "I wanted a dog that nobody else wanted. I've always been like that. I've always wanted the animals nobody else wanted. I wanted to be useful. This was something good that I could do."

In the shelter that day was a beautiful white husky that Maria was sure would be adopted soon, but also a large, intimidating three-to-four-year-old rottweiler-shepherd mix who had been in the kennel for nearly a year. Maria feared that Frieda might be put down if she was not adopted soon.

The shelter workers had named the dog ACC because she had roamed the grounds of Adirondack Community College for a year before a student contacted the shelter. Then it had taken them nearly a year to catch her.

Hundreds, if not thousands, of people had seen ACC in the shelter and decided not to adopt her. For one thing, the two breeds in her makeup—rottweilers and shepherds—both have a reputation for being aggressive. People found Frieda unnerving. She was a large dog, with a keen hunting instinct, and she had a challenging stare, big, scary teeth, and a formidable demeanor.

For Maria, it was a simple decision. She remembers looking at Frieda—who sat still, looking quietly back at her—and thinking that she was just adorable. This makes me smile, because even though I've grown to love Frieda, "adorable" is not a word I would ever use to describe her.

Maria never saw Frieda as menacing, then or now. This, I reflected upon hearing the story, was probably a good harbinger for me. Maria had a high tolerance for craziness, and a fondness for animals and people other people avoided. Maybe she would one day find *me* cute.

Mostly, Maria's decision came down to her reasoning that the husky would get adopted and ACC wouldn't. So she took her home. Inspired by the dog's distinctive eyebrows, she renamed her Frieda as a tribute to the Mexican artist Frida Kahlo, who'd had famously dark and luxuriant eyebrows.

Before we met, but not too long after Maria got Frieda, I too got a new dog. I went to meet a breeder, Gretchen Pinkel, and decided to get Lenore, the black Lab I dubbed "the Hound of Love." The way I got Lenore could not be more different from the way Maria got Frieda.

I spent months researching Labrador retrievers, reading books and other materials and talking extensively with trainers and breeders. This was followed by hours visiting Lenore's breeder, seeing her dogs, discussing my needs and wishes, comparing our philosophies of dogs, pondering the implications for my writing life, and then, after more visits and consultations, I finally decided on Lenore, who was eight weeks old. She came from a much decorated and grounded line of prize-winning Labs, and had never skipped a meal or worried about one in her life.

Just before I met Maria, I was beginning my tailspin into a nearly total breakdown. My marriage was falling apart, and my long history of avoiding responsibility for my own life was starting to have devastating consequences. I had become disconnected from my world, my family, my life.

I did not go to a therapist, not yet. Instead, I went to a breeder in Argyle, New York. I did the same thing Maria did, yet in a completely different way.

I got Lenore. And she was very different from Frieda. She really was adorable.

Lenore changed a lot of things in my life, especially my intellectualized idea about dogs. She stole my heart and shattered my detachment, and more than anything else, she kept love and the idea of love alive for me.

Alone on the farm, with my marriage dissolving, veering toward bankruptcy and collapse, I was living as unhealthy a life as one could live. You don't see too many movies about sixty-year-old men rebuilding their lives and finding love, and especially not while isolated on a remote farm in the country. I had dug the biggest hole for myself, and unsurprisingly, I had just fallen into it.

It is difficult to sort out all of the different impulses that explain why we do the things we do. In the years before I came to Bedlam Farm, my writing career was foundering. I wasn't sure what to write about. I wanted to learn more about animals, so I got donkeys, cows, goats, chickens, barn cats. But my focus was dogs. I found myself drawn to working dogs, dogs who would want to do things with me and help me explore the human-animal bond. Dogs who could go places, behave appropriately, accompany me to readings, share my life, be safe. Dogs I did not have to worry about. Dogs that were not Frieda.

I was fascinated by dogs, and by the intense ways in which people attached to them. It was a subject that drew me powerfully as a writer, and that I suspected could never be exhausted. Some literary critics sniff and grump about the proliferation of dog books, wondering why there are so many. I have always wondered why there aren't more. Americans own more than seventy-four million dogs, according to the Humane Society, and people love them more than ever.

Maria's needs and approach were very different from mine. She wanted to save and nurture something. She wanted the companion that the lonely and fearful child yearns for. As analyst Dorothy Burlingham wrote, "The child takes an imaginary animal as his intimate and beloved companion; subsequently he is never separated from his animal friend, and in this way he overcomes loneliness." The animal, she adds, "offers the child what he is searching for: faithful love and unswerving devotion. There's nothing that this dumb animal cannot understand. Speech is quite unnecessary, for understanding comes without words."

Maria brought Skunk to the shelter, and the workers there brought Frieda out to them. The two dogs sniffed each other warily but seemed to get along. The next day Maria called the shelter and said she would take Frieda home. When she arrived, they brought the dog out on a leash and collected the $75 fee. Maria signed the adoption papers and put Frieda in her Toyota. Much later, a shelter worker would tell me they had given up on Frieda ever being adopted, and they were desperate for space. She didn't have much longer.

Maria remembers that Frieda defecated and vomited the entire way home, and it was the worst mess she had ever seen. It seemed like Frieda had never been in a car before. When they got to the house, Frieda went off into a corner and slept.

When she awoke, she was Maria's dog, as simple as that.

We like to think we know everything about dogs, but we don't. Frieda, who was suspicious of everyone, who had to know someone for months before she would take a biscuit from them, trusted Maria and attached to her instantly and completely, and there is no one in the animal universe who can really say why this powerful soul connection was made. Rottweilers and German shepherds are both notoriously loyal and protective breeds. Frieda had found her mission in life. There was a great need inside of both of them, and each saw it in the other.

Maria recalls that Frieda was very quiet the first few days, rarely barking or growling. She had a brawl or two with Skunk, but the two dogs worked it out. Frieda followed Maria everywhere, watched her closely, obeyed her as long as no strangers or new dogs were around. And Maria quickly learned to make sure there were no strangers or dogs around when Frieda went out. She never brought Frieda to work at the houses she was helping restore, as she couldn't trust her to be safe. So Frieda stayed in the house all day, barking at mail carriers, trucks, bicyclists, and anything else that went by.

Maria also remembers being concerned that Frieda was almost too quiet those first few days in the house. Clever girl, she was just adapting. The real Frieda—the terror—emerged shortly, when she busted through the front door and nearly ran down a pickup truck with a loud engine.

From the first, there was a schizophrenic quality about her. As explosive as she could sometimes be outside, inside the house she followed Maria everywhere and did what she was told.

And then, as so often happens when people get dogs whose backgrounds are unknown or unknowable, Maria began learning things about Frieda:

- That Frieda was fiercely protective of Maria and their home, throwing herself at doors and windows when anybody came near.

- That Frieda was untrained and responded to few, if any, commands.

- That she didn't like other dogs, especially small ones, or female ones, or dogs that moved fast. All of these she would try to run down and eat.

- That she loved to chase motorcycles, ATVs, and trucks.

- That she was a fierce hunter who would take off in a flash after chipmunks, raccoons, skunks, and deer. And, often, catch them.

- That she had a powerful sense of boundaries—she patrolled doors, windows, and fences like a Special Forces sentry dog. That was her job: to keep the world out.

The main thing Maria noticed was that Frieda was very protective of her, and partly as a result, she became very protective of Frieda.

One Sunday, Maria brought Frieda to her mother's house for a family dinner. Her nieces and nephews were there. Frieda was lying on a bed in a guest room when one of the girls reached over to stroke her belly. Suddenly, Frieda snapped at her hand. She didn't bite the girl, though she easily could have. She didn't even growl a warning. It seemed a split-second, defensive reflex. The kids were okay with it, but Maria wasn't. It was a fateful moment for Frieda. After that, Frieda was kept away from all children and stayed in the bedroom by herself during family dinners.

She was kept away from most adults, too. Maria is not one of those people who can turn a blind eye to the possibility that her dog might harm or maim someone. It was not a risk she was willing to take, despite her great love for her dog.

Like many people who find themselves with difficult dogs, Maria's response was emotional, loving. But also confining. She stopped taking Frieda places, stopped socializing her. Maria doesn't have it in herself to hurt or frighten anyone or anything, and she made sure that Frieda would never again have the chance to nip at a kid, or run down an ATV, or attack another dog. If she couldn't bear the thought of Frieda dying alone in a shelter, nor could she bear the thought of Frieda hurting another living thing or being hurt herself.

Training was never conducted in the places it was perhaps the most necessary—out in the world. I wasn't there, but I suspect Frieda was reinforced in the idea that she had to keep the world away. She was successful. The world stayed away.

So Frieda froze in place, with all of her troubles. She obeyed Maria inside the house and kept close to her on walks, as long as she was on a leash. And from that point on, she was almost always on a leash. Maria had no fear of Frieda, and Frieda was nothing but affectionate to her. She left the world, and her bond with Maria grew tighter. With dogs like Frieda, either they get out into the world and become socialized or they have to be withdrawn from the world and find it confusing and alien, something to be kept out. Maria didn't really have much time to train Frieda—her job required long hours and was physically draining. And she didn't really know how to train a dog as wild as Frieda. Most people don't. The drama of dog rescue is that it is sometimes hard and difficult work. People get dogs whose backgrounds are murky, and often they simply conclude that the animals were abused or mistreated and leave it at that.

Frieda was kept from failing. But she was also not given a chance to succeed.

You can't look at a human-dog relationship and not consider the context in which it occurs. Maria had long suffered from anxiety and depression, much of it swirling around her aborted life as an artist, and she had largely withdrawn from the world, in just the way Frieda now did. She acknowledged that she was in hiding. She had no computer or cellphone, and very little contact beyond a small circle of friends.

Maria was seeking a friend she could trust, one who might protect her from an alien and sometimes frightening world. Frieda was looking for work, and her work seemed to be watching over and protecting a human who needed her.

In a way, Frieda owes her life to the very curious ways in which Americans choose their dogs.

Normally, we make hardheaded, rational decisions about what comes into our homes and lives—houses, cars, appliances, furniture. We carefully consider things like price, reviews, warranties and guarantees, a company's track record. Nobody wants a sofa that's going to fall apart in a few years or a toaster that doesn't brown the bread. We pore over online sales histories and ratings, weighing our purchases thoughtfully and grilling salespeople mercilessly.

But when it comes to an unpredictable animal entering our homes and sharing a life with us and our kids for many years, the decision is often emotional, visceral, from the heart, not the mind.

In America, the notion of how to help people has become politically charged and bitterly divisive, like so many things. We seem to feel as a culture that it isn't really our job to help flawed humans; they have to help themselves.

Helping animals is not controversial. This work seems acceptable, culturally and politically, across the spectrum of age, race, income, gender. Helping animals is much simpler, a quicker way to feel good and to do good, at least in theory.

To many people, acquiring a dog has become a moral decision. There are lots of dogs in need, so the proper thing to do is bring one of them home. When people tell me they are getting a dog, I always ask how. "Oh, from a shelter, of course," most people respond, as if any other option were unthinkable. Or they say, "I'm not spending money on a dog," which to me is a baffling way to think about bringing an animal into one's home for years, often to live with children, as opposed to, let's say, a sofa, or a $1,500 backyard barbecue grill, or a $3,000 HDTV.

Many dogs pay for this curious approach with their lives, returned to shelters or euthanized when morality (feeling good) conflicts with reality—peeing, barking, chewing, biting, expensive vet bills.

Getting a dog that way is a crapshoot, a gamble. But sometimes this chaotic and random process works, and it works so well it is almost beyond imagination. Sometimes, a person in need meets a dog in need and the two of them fit together like missing pieces of a puzzle, their lives melding seamlessly and powerfully. I like to say that if we are lucky, we get the dog we need. And that if a dog is lucky, he finds the human of his dreams and needs.

I have avoided dogs like Frieda because they are intimidating and, if not carefully trained, unpredictable. Certain breeds—pit bulls, German shepherds, rottweilers—are widely feared in much of America. This is partly because of the disproportionate media attention these breeds get when they injure somebody. Labrador retrievers are much more likely to bite people than rottweilers or pit bulls, yet they are simply not as frightening to people, and they also tend to do less damage when they do get aggressive.

I know that these stereotypes are simplistic and unfair. Pit bulls and rottweilers can be the most loyal and safe dogs to be around. Yet sometimes bad people get good dogs, and for the rest of the population, there is no simple way to know who is who.

I take my dogs to public appearances and readings, and I can't afford to be surprised by anything they do. While I have always had rescue dogs—Orson, Izzy, two other border collies who were rehomed—I also feel that getting a dog from a good breeder is one of the most satisfying and successful experiences in the human-animal spectrum. For me, getting a dog is not a moral decision but a practical one. Not a way of making me feel good about my morality, but about getting a dog that can live comfortably and safely in my life. It's an increasingly minority view.

Our cultural notions of dogs and how to get them have changed over the years. A lot.

I grew up with a German shepherd named King. King lived in the pre-sensitivity, pre-lawsuit, pre–culture of fear era of American life. King did not eat dog food. My mother would have been horrified at the notion of buying food for a dog. (I often wonder what she would think of the twenty-five-pound bags of imported holistic dog food priced at $74 I see in the pet stores. Or how some people consider feeding table scraps to a dog abusive.) What King didn't get from us, he fished out of the neighborhood trash bins.

My father did not walk around after King with a plastic bag to pick up King's poop. King would not have lasted long if he had.

King did not go to the vet, not once in his life. If the dog got into a fight or cut himself, he got a Band-Aid, just like the rest of us.

King did not wear a collar or walk on a leash. Ever.

In the morning, my mother opened the door and let King out to roam our working-class neighborhood in Providence, Rhode Island. He often terrorized children on their way to school, tore apart our neighbors' garbage, scattered it on lawns, brought some home. Every morning, alerted by the clanging of milk bottles, he took off after the milkman, who would usually, but not always, make it back to his truck in time.

Several times a year, King would get the postman and tear off a chunk of his pants, or worse. My parents would pay for a new pair. I never heard anyone mention legal action, although, in retrospect, King seems to me like a lawsuit on four paws.

King was not neutered, and the idea would have seemed absurd to my parents. A dog's sex life was not something we worried about. He roamed the neighborhood, chasing after his girlfriends, having sex, and routinely impregnating the neighbors' dogs. There were little Kings all over the neighborhood. I was afraid of King, who would often growl at me, or nip me if I tried to touch him. I didn't often try.

In the evening, my mother would open the back door, yell "King!," and leave out scraps from dinner. King would appear mysteriously, eat his food in the backyard, and then come into the basement to sleep.

Times have certainly changed. If I saw a dog like King today, I would probably report his family to Animal Control. Not only would most of this behavior now be considered illegal; I would deem it neglect or abuse, and so does the law.

To the end of their days, my mother and father talked about King, about how much they loved him, what a great dog he was, and what great dog lovers they were.

I remember my mother meeting one of my dogs at some point and smiling (I never saw her actually touch a dog). "We loved our dogs so much," she said sadly. "I really miss having one."

Our life with King was not unusual. Most of the dogs in the neighborhood lived that way. Dogs mirror life, really, and their lives mirror the times in which they live.

King was hit by cars several times, and when this happened, he was let into the basement to recover. Mostly, he did, although he had a distinct limp. One day, King never came home, a not uncommon occurrence then in the lives of dogs. We learned later—from a neighbor who'd been passing by at the time—that he was hit by a truck he was chasing, and sanitation workers came to haul away his body.

My parents did not want to claim the body, or bury it. Nor was there any grieving I could remember. Two weeks later, they went out and adopted another dog at the pound (as shelters were called back then). Sam, a basset hound who had been found roaming the streets of East Providence, cost one dollar. My parents were not asked any questions about how he would be kept, sheltered, or fed. They just took him home.

Nobody can trace the nearly unfathomable chemical, emotional, and biological factors that cause some dogs and some people to find each other and bond. It is a ballet of love, circumstance, psychology, and need. Our lives with these creatures is, after all, a dance we embrace almost intuitively and instinctively but are rarely called upon to understand, at least not in the moment.

When I met Maria and Frieda that warm, sunny day in the barn, I had joined the dance, although I didn't know it then. I had no idea that Frieda would enter my life and alter it in the most profound way, but that's one of the beautiful things about animals. They change you, and you almost never see it coming. There are people who say they knew right away when they saw a dog that it was meant for them.

I am not one of those people. I generally grasp that the train is coming just before it plows right into me.

Chapter Three

The Studio Barn

When I tell people my friendship with Maria began in barns, they look at me a little funny. We first met in a barn she was restoring, but the real turning point in our friendship—the place where the plot thickens—was in another barn, one of the four barns on Bedlam Farm, the one we called the "studio barn."

After our first meetings, I hadn't really expected to see much of Maria again, but I kept thinking of her and her crazy dog.

Although she seemed almost painfully shy to me, and very guarded, she caught my attention. I barely knew her, yet I felt completely at ease with her. I could always make her laugh, and she had the most radiant smile.

It was a point in my life where I was uncomfortable with almost everyone, even my own family. Yet I was so comfortable around this stranger, this nomad who moved from house to house, restoring and bringing beauty to old and dilapidated structures. Who didn't have a computer or a cellphone. Who was an artist who made no art.

I didn't want to lose this friendship.

Several weeks after we met, I called and invited her and her husband to dinner. She agreed, and so we began the first phase of our relationship—friends with similar sensibilities, living in the country, having dinner at a local tavern. Casual conversation, banter about politics, about living in the country. I heard my first stories of Frieda, how she could not be near dogs or people. How she had to be walked at night, out in the woods. How fearful Maria was that she would frighten people, harm other dogs, so much so that she would not invite many people to their home.

At this point we became dinner friends, couple friends. Every so often, Maria and I and her husband, plus my wife when she was visiting, would get together. Maria and I do not care much for politics, but our spouses did, and so the conversation would often turn to that. We talked about their work, restorations; my work, book writing; and my wife's work, teaching and journalism. From the beginning, Maria and I did most of our important talking together, not out at dinners with family or friends. Neither of us felt comfortable talking about our art among them, or seeking encouragement.

At these dinners, Maria didn't say much; she deferred: to me, to her husband, to others. She was always the quietest person at the table; she said the least. People would argue about politics, get upset about the left or the right, but when other voices rose, hers became silent. I would ask her questions to draw her out, and I soon began to see the warmth and openness that underlay her cautious veneer. And she was funny, I discovered. She had a quick, wicked sense of humor and often ribbed me about contradictions between what I said and what I wrote.

I told her once at dinner that I didn't embrace much of the "spiritual mumbo jumbo" about animals and people. She just smiled, but her eyes flashed. "Well, one day I'll get a video of you singing to Lenore and put it up on YouTube, and we'll let everybody see what a hard-ass you really are."

She had a gift for putting me in my place, and the odd thing was that I always needed that, knew it was good for me.

We talked about animals, artists we knew, books we were reading. We were often in our own side conversations, neither of us wanting to argue about the stories on the news, the outrages of the day. I always wished I could just sit down with her alone, and I always had the feeling she did, too. She seemed to always expect trouble to break out, and she always tried to steer the conversation to safe topics.

It went on like that for months, but I had been a reporter for a long time, a good one, and I began to put pieces of the puzzle together.

It was very clear to me that she loved Frieda as much as she loved anything in the world, that they were somehow two refugees clinging to the same raft. And that she was an artist in her heart and soul, and that she pined for her art and the making of it. And that she was gentle and loving. I saw that she needed a lot of wine at the end of every day. I saw that there was something inside her that wanted to come out.

It was nice for both of us to find a friend, but that was all we expected, and we were grateful for it.

It's easy to see now that I was drawn to her, but at the time, it seemed very random and natural. We were "just friends," but we were friends with a deep connection. Without consulting each other or saying a word about it, we were very careful about the time we spent together. Our conversations had boundaries. Frieda was always a safe subject. We could talk about her, discuss her training, quite easily. She was the first thing we shared.

When you move upstate from a place like New York City, you learn quickly that you will never be seen by the locals as being local. Generally, your home is never known by your name, but by the name of the last "local" who lived there. Ralph Keyes was the farmer who built the studio barn. And whenever anybody asks me where my farm is, I always say, "It's the old Keyes place," and everybody knows. It's hard for me to imagine my farm ever being referred to as "the old Katz place."

Bedlam Farm is situated on about ninety acres in a remote chunk of upstate New York a couple of hours northeast of Albany. The farm was built in 1861 by a carpenter and businessman named James Patterson. Patterson ran a mill, raised pigs and cows, grew potatoes, and had various business interests. The big barn was probably the first building to be constructed on this sharply sloping hillside, beautifully sited with a view of West Hebron and, beyond it, the Green Mountains of Vermont. The farmhouse Patterson built in 1861 was grand by the standards of the time. Multiple additions were added over the years, and now it sprawls, with a big living room with beautiful high ceilings on one end and a large woodshed, now a family room, on the other.

Around the farmhouse, almost in a circle, are four barns: the big dairy barn, which housed cows and hay; the carriage barn, where the horses and buggies were kept; a pig barn, where the farm's pigs were slaughtered; and an odd little clapboard building called the studio barn. This is the ugly duckling of my barns, more a large shed than a barn, really.

In the front of the farmhouse is a wooden fence, backed by wire mesh, where my dogs often sit and look out at the world. Behind the farmhouse is another, more secure fenced-in area originally built for goats and donkeys, now used when we want to put the dogs out and don't want to worry about them digging a tunnel or leaping to freedom, two ever-present concerns with border collies.

Across from the farmhouse, and by the carriage barn, a beautiful old dirt path leads nearly a mile into the deep woods. It is where I've walked the dogs ever since I moved to Washington County.

One day back in 2003, I was driving along Route 30 when I looked up and saw this old farm sitting up on the hill. I called a real estate agent and said I wanted to buy it. I didn't know why, really; I just felt I needed to be there, to live my life and do my work as a writer. I had never really spent time on a farm; I'm not sure I had ever set foot on one before. However, I sensed, rather than thought, that this would be a wondrous laboratory in which to explore my ideas about dogs and other animals, and to write about rural life, which fascinated me. And eventually I came to know why I was running so far away from my life in New Jersey.

Without really understanding it, I had embarked on what Joseph Campbell calls the hero's journey. I would learn the perils and joys of the pilgrim who sets out to find the meaning of his own life, and to live it. Maria and Frieda were setting out as well, and it was in this ugly little studio barn—built as an appliance repair shop by a struggling farmer—that the three of us would collide.

In January 2008, I offered Maria the use of the studio barn, a gesture that was to alter our lives in ways neither of us had considered. Maria was trained as an artist, and she worked with discarded fiber material. She made quilts, mostly, and dresses and scarves. She had not worked as an artist for more than a decade, something that filled her eyes with sadness whenever she mentioned it.

Maria is not a person who takes things easily, or ever asks for them. She did not trust many people, particularly men. When I offered her the studio barn, she looked as if she had been struck by a lightning bolt.

She was quiet for a while.

"I can't take that—it's your barn," she said, so quietly I almost didn't hear her.

I told her the barn was empty, that I had been looking for a good and creative use of it.

"I would love to have it, to use it," she blurted. "I can't take it for free."

Then she said she would think about it. She wasn't sure. But I saw the gleam in her eyes, and I sensed that she badly wanted to have this space of her own.

Since I had four barns and was using only one, I had thought nothing of offering her the use of this space. Unlike the other barns, it had heat—though not much—and water. I had been thinking of tearing it down. Offering it to Maria didn't seem like a big deal.

I had this fantasy that the farm would become an inspirational place for creative people, a place of community and support. Life in upstate New York is rough in some ways, and encouragement can be hard to come by. People have other things to worry about. I had always craved the idea of encouragement but had not often received much. So I felt the power of it.

Maria thought about my offer, hemmed and hawed, struggled with the idea. She eventually came back and said she would love to use the barn, provided that I would let her help with farm chores and animal care on the weekends. She wouldn't take the studio space for free. Even better, I thought. At the time, the farm was beginning its rapid descent into chaos: there were sheep, donkeys, goats, chickens, barn cats, two Swiss steers and a dairy cow, plus three dogs. I had a tractor, and work crews were tearing up the house, the barn, the grounds. I was losing control, and felt exhausted and frightened. I was thrilled at the idea of Maria coming around on weekends to help out. She could come for only a little while, she said, on Saturday and Sunday mornings. She would check the water and the hay.

"You've got a deal," I told her. For me, it was a big deal, the biggest deal, my own Louisiana Purchase.

I think on some level we were both instinctively worried

about how Maria's presence on the farm might look to other people, so without any discussion, we observed strict boundaries.

I never knew when Maria was coming to the studio barn, and she never told me.

On weekends, Maria would show up early in the morning, her pockets stuffed with carrots and apples for the animals; she would haul out the hay and check the water.

Maria reminded me of a skittish deer. She was quiet, introspective, even brooding. But she had a striking rapport with the animals. She loved them all, even the sheep, whom I found exasperating, and the chickens, who also left me cold. She brought food for them all, talked to each one, knelt down and looked them all in the eye. She had a word for everybody, and she spoke in a calm, soothing voice that made the animals feel comfortable and safe. Me, too. I found that she was a real animal lover, that she had the gift of communicating with them, making them comfortable. She was never afraid of them or nervous around them.

If I ran into her, she would say good morning, look away, and then leave. She never initiated a conversation or joined in one, unless it was to tell me an animal was limping or looked ill. "Mute" was the word that kept coming to mind when I thought of her. She just seemed to have no voice.

She also had a creative streak that was evident in her clothes and her speech (on the few occasions when she could not avoid conversation). She always noticed color and texture, spotted a beautiful flower, appreciated the quality of light, the mist in the field. She was clearly artistic, but she had not been making art for some time, and a great sadness swirled around her. Vulnerability and pain just seemed to radiate from her, but she never spoke about it. Having her own space meant the world to her; that was obvious. And she would soon be making her art, something she so clearly ached to do.

As always, Frieda hovered like a ghost, even if she wasn't present.

Maria never brought Frieda to the barn or to the farm. It was just understood. She rarely brought Frieda anywhere, she was so worried about someone getting hurt.

I was glad about that. Sometimes Frieda was in the car when Maria came by. Once or twice she walked up the hill with Frieda. It was never a pleasant or encouraging experience. The sight of my dogs made Frieda crazy, and she nearly foamed at the mouth trying to get at them.

A few days later, deep in the night, I heard some sounds outside and I looked out my bedroom window. The studio barn was lit up like a freighter on the seas. I could see a shadow flitting across the new blinds that had been put up—sheets of colorful fabric. I could hear music drifting softly across the road.

Lenore was listening too, looking out from her vantage point at the foot of the bed. "Look, Lenore, listen," I said, and Lenore's tail began thumping. I was crying for joy. I could only imagine what this gifted and endearing and vulnerable human across the road was feeling.

In January 2008, while Maria was restarting her life as an artist, mine was unraveling. I was in a dark and lonely place, disconnected from my family and my past. I saw a therapist. "I don't want to end my life like this," I told her. "Then don't," she replied.

So I decided I would not. I would do whatever I had to do to find love and peace in my life, even if there might be only a few days left of it. I would not live a life bounded by fear.

My therapist told me that I was not really married anymore, and the truth of this statement brought my world down around me.

I was, in fact, married and had been for thirty-five years, but I had come to the farm by myself, and was alone there most of the time. When I realized my marriage was coming to an end, I broke down. I remember looking at a big bag of dog food and thinking that I was just like that bag after the string on the top had been pulled. I had spilled out.

I stopped sleeping, started vomiting, sweating, fending off one panic attack after another, talking in circles. I didn't have many friends, and the ones I had quickly vanished, and who can blame them? What an awful mess I was.

As a child, I'd been paralyzed by fear, and I'd figured out early that if I gave the fear to other people, and let them run my life, I wouldn't have to worry so much about it. Now that was no longer possible, and it was fear's turn to run amok in my life. I was like a five-year-old boy suddenly finding himself with a book contract and a farm to run. Except I was sixty. The boy and the man needed to get to know each other, and fast.

I had a lot of work to do.

Most nights during this period, I went out on hospice visits with my border collie Izzy, whom I had trained as a therapy dog. The work was satisfying and meaningful, but not the path to normal health and connection. Still, there is no better way to gain perspective on your own self-absorption and self-pity than sitting down and holding the hand of someone who has only a few days or hours to live.

There is no need to go into all of the details of my crack-up, except to say that I did not think I would survive it, and almost did not, and that I would never have survived it without Maria. An analyst told me that he had never seen a man my age undertake so much change at once. He wished me good luck with it and wrote me a prescription for sleeping pills and anti-anxiety medication. "Oh," he said, "and try meditation. It might change your life."

I had never conceived of so much loneliness, confusion, and fear. My fear turned obsessive, and I couldn't write or think or focus much. I didn't get a good night's sleep for nearly three years.

The one thing I could focus on was Maria. Starting in the middle of the week, usually on Wednesdays, I would begin counting the hours until Maria would walk through the back door of the farmhouse to get the cat food. I understand now that I kept the cat food in the pantry so that Maria would have a reason to come into the farmhouse. She arrived at the same time every Saturday morning—seven-thirty—and stayed for about ten minutes, bringing hay out to the donkeys and the goats, checking on their water, feeding the barn cats.

Wednesday night, when I got into bed, I would tell myself that I would be okay that night, because in fifty-seven hours and fifteen minutes, Maria would come in the door and I could talk with her, perhaps offer her some tea, if she could stay, which she rarely did. In bed, I breathed. I prayed. I sweated. I visualized and meditated, counting numbers and kicking balls of fear over imaginary fields. I waited for Maria.

And here's the thing: she always walked through the door. Always. As I lost control of my mind and, sometimes, my body, I clung every day to one image, one idea: Maria would always come through the door. If she did not, then there was no hope, no promise. Sometimes I cried when I heard her car pull into the driveway. Sometimes I cried when she left. As I write this now, I could easily cry again. Maria always came through the door. She always will. When nobody else on the earth came through the door, she did.

All week, I would count down, count down, count down. I didn't know where I kept my pants, but I knew to the second when Maria was coming.

Saturday mornings I would be in the kitchen, the kettle steaming, and I would hear the dogs bark or the pasture fence creak, and I would take as deep a breath as I could, and the world would stop spinning for a second or two. Then, after she fed the donkeys, gave treats to the sheep, checked on the water, I would hear her boots crunching in the ice behind the house and she would come into the kitchen and smile at me, and the sun would come up and light up the world.

If she noticed me mumbling, talking to myself, dropping the teacups and the tea bags, she never said. Much later, I asked her if she had been put off by my strange behavior, and she said she just didn't think much about it.

Sometimes she stayed for tea for ten minutes or so; usually she didn't. I wanted so badly for her to call and check up on me, but I knew she couldn't do that, and I couldn't ask her to. Still, the sight of her was enough to get me through the weekend.

Maria and I first met in 2007, and our friendship-turned-romance, from first encounter to marriage, spanned about four years. For the first year, neither of us ever imagined we would be divorced. Certainly, that delusion is what made it safe for us to be together. She never once mentioned or discussed her marriage, and she completely bought the story I told and wrote—that my wife and I were a modern couple supporting each other in our need to live apart. It was a good story, and I believed it. Some people did not. Every year I went on a book tour, and every year my readers told me that they saw how lonely I was and wondered when the myth of the "separate but together" marriage would crumble. How humbling for a writer of memoir to hear that, again and again.

Maria and I rarely saw each other apart from her weekly visits to the farm. Then I started taking photographs, which she had always encouraged me to do. I had never taken a photograph in my life until I ordered my Canon online and started driving around with my border collie Izzy in the bitter cold, chasing sunsets. I would come up to a hill, see the lowering sun and sky, and pull over. It was insanely foolish to wander around country roads at dusk like that. My car door was hit once, my tripod zinged by a speeding truck, and countless times I dove for the side of the road. Perhaps I wanted to go that way. I was seized by the light and the sky, by the colors. I couldn't wait to get home and see what I'd caught, marvel at the colors, put the photos up on my blog.

Something inside me was beginning to open up, beginning

to understand what it means to be an artist, to have something so powerful and beautiful bottled up and literally dying to come out.

I know now that every photo I have ever taken is a love letter to Maria. At that time, there were two things it was okay for us to talk about: Frieda and my photographs. Because Maria was an artist, I valued her feedback, and because she was an artist, it seemed appropriate for her to give it. I loved taking photos, and she could not resist talking to me about them. The photos were our language, our way of talking. She has seen every photo I have ever taken, and she always tells me how good they are—or aren't.

I was always looking for ways to talk to Maria, to connect with her. I encouraged her to pursue her art; she encouraged me in my writing and my photography. We decided to coproduce a small art show at nearby Gardenworks, a farm and garden center—*An Art Harvest,* we called it. We would present our own work, as well as the works of several other artists we wanted to encourage. One of them was and is very special to us. She is one of the few people in our lives to have borne witness to our friendship, our struggles, and our love, and who provided so much support when we most needed it.

In 2006, I had received a letter from a woman named Mary Kellogg, who wrote that she and a group of friends had been planning excursions together for more than half a century. This year, they wanted to see Bedlam Farm. Would that be possible? she asked.

I had the most wonderful time with these women. We

herded the sheep, toured the barns, ate lunch, and sat on the porch. Mary and I took to each other, and we became friends. Mary says in her blunt way that she didn't like me as much then as she does now, that I was always busy and distracted. I know this is true.

Mary told me on the porch one day that she was a poet, that she had written poetry ever since she was eleven years old (she was seventy-eight when we met) and had never shown it to anyone. I asked to read her poems. She let me. I loved them.

I had never met anyone like Mary. She seemed to have escaped from a Norman Rockwell portrait of some other America. She was beautiful even as she neared eighty. Ramrod straight, honest, fiercely independent. She didn't go to doctors much, mowed her own lawn, planted her own garden. "Some of the ladies tell me I should move to someplace easier to maintain," she would chuckle. "Not for me."

No, it wasn't. On Mother's Day, Mary would take off with a friend for a drive so as not to bother her kids. She helped run her church, brought food to the poor and soup to the elderly, took hikes, worked for hours planting flowers, writing her poems, reading. Her husband, Dick, had died more than a decade ago. I knew she missed him terribly, but I got that only from her poems. She did not complain about life.

Mary lived on a thirty-acre farm in North Hebron that was even more remote than mine. After Dick died, Mary wasn't interested in downsizing to fulfill America's dwindling expectations of the aged. She was active in the community, helped a local hospice facility get funded and built, visited her friends and her daughters and grandkids. And she wrote her poems.

If it snowed heavily, I'd call her. She was always fine. Somebody would plow her out, or she'd just stay inside and watch the birds come to the feeders and write some poems or make some jam.

In the country, life happens. Phones go dead. Roofs collapse, water pipes burst. Mary handled all of it, and by herself. She did not ask for help, or need much.

I learned very quickly not to patronize Mary, as we so often do with older people. During one awful ice storm, I called her up to see if she was all right. I couldn't walk ten feet from the house, let alone drive. She said she was fine.

An hour later, there was a knock on the back door. Mary was standing there in her parka and rain hat, holding a giant vat of warm soup.

"I thought you might need some food," she said. "I know you fall down all the time out here." I thanked her and took the soup. She drove off. I never again called Mary to ask how she was doing in a storm.

We became close friends, talked on the phone, visited with each other. One summer afternoon I went to her house, high on a mountaintop a mile from the nearest neighbor, and Mary nearly ran me over in the tractor she was driving to mow her vast lawn. Mary had the gift of being content with who she was. She was never idle, and although she clearly missed Dick, she was rarely lonely.

Attachment theory, I have learned, isn't only for people and animals. It explains many of the things we do. My experience with Mary helped me see how important encouragement was for me—how much I needed it, how much I wanted to offer it. It was to be such a big part of my life upstate—as well as of my blog and my books. And it was the genesis of my relationship with Maria.

I was touched by the image of this gifted older woman writing her poetry, and keeping her work hidden for so long. I thought it would be wonderful if Mary's poems were published. With just a little bit of encouragement, she had gathered them and agreed to work with me on a book of poetry. At the same time, I was beginning to understand how the artist in Maria had to come out if she was to emerge from the dark place she was in. She had lost faith in her art, in her ability to make it and in the willingness of anyone else to see it or buy it.

Mary taught me that if you can encourage people in healthy ways, you can get them started and they will take it from there. This idea evolved, became the foundation of my love for Maria and hers for me. It was the first big idea we shared.

Maria seemed to me like a fragile seed then; just a little bit of water and sun seemed to bring her out, light her up, give her strength. She buoyed me as well. Mary opened my eyes to the power of encouragement, and it was the beginning of love for me, and for Maria.

I've tried to help people in various ways—some healthy, some destructive—but I think it was through Mary that I learned how to do it properly. To encourage people without taking on their problems or interfering with their lives.

I talked to Maria about this project, and she was as enthusiastic as I was. We began having morning meetings at the farm with Mary to plan the book, and I asked Maria if she would agree to edit it, as she had come to love Mary as much as I did.

Now we had a reason to talk on the phone, to have lunch

occasionally, even take trips to Troy to meet with the publisher who would print five hundred copies of Mary's first collection of poems, *My Place on Earth,* which included a score or more of my photographs.

I understood that poetry doesn't sell much, and I expected to lose the cost of printing the books. As usual, I had underestimated Mary. The book is in its fifth printing and has earned a small profit. Mary sold most of those copies by herself.

Mary's poems cemented my friendship with Maria. And Mary was the first witness to our relationship, seeing everything, missing nothing. She and Maria quickly became close, and they kept an eye on each other. And on me.

Maria was anxious about taking the project on. She had never edited a book before, and, as usual, she doubted she could do it, but I told her that her artistic sense and instincts for design were all she needed, and this was true. She was a natural, choosing and organizing the photographs, gently pulling poems out of Mary, meeting with the publisher and making the right decisions. She just didn't know her own gifts.

I can see now that Maria and I were always projecting our own creative yearnings onto others, and onto each other. We wanted to encourage Mary for sure, but we also wanted to encourage ourselves. I would drive with Maria to Troy every few weeks. We would talk, laugh, stop at Dunkin' Donuts for coffee and muffins. I saw then how easily we talked to each other, how comfortable we were together, what good friends we were. Maria, I thought, would always be my pal. I had never really had a best friend before. I loved it.

One morning, we both were sitting in the farmhouse living room after Maria and Mary and I had met to plan the production of her book. I am not good at design, so I'd left this to Maria, and I was startled at how well she did, how easily she took to it, how confident she was about the way the book and the photos ought to be melded together. I'm not good at production, but I've been through the process on enough books of my own to know a good design when I see one, and her skill was astonishing, especially for someone who had never done it. Watching her with Mary, I was taken with how confident she seemed, how often she laughed. I was looking at a different version of Maria or, perhaps, I thought, at the real one.

So I was surprised during this particular meeting, after Mary had left, to glance over and see Maria sitting on the floor, tears streaming down her face.

"What's wrong?" I asked.

She shook her head a few times, as if she didn't want to speak of it, and then said, "I'm no good at this. I just don't know what I'm doing. I'm sorry to be screwing it up."

We had a long talk that morning, perhaps our first real and serious talk. I told her she had done a great job, that she was a natural at this creative packaging, and that Mary and I were thrilled with her work. After a few minutes, she looked up at me and asked, "Are you just saying that?"

And we both started laughing. You see, the thing is, Maria and I, two people who had learned not to believe very many people, always believed each other, always. Maria said this was the first time in her life that anyone had told her that.

Publishing *My Place on Earth* was one of the most satisfying experiences of my life. Maria and I did it together, which was wonderful, and it lifted me up to see how much people loved Mary's poems. Mary was very happy to see her work out in the world. And Maria and I had helped her to do it. Wow, did that feel good.

And it emboldened me. I began to urge Maria to believe in herself, to push aside the past. To make her art and bring it out into the world. "If Mary could do it," I'd say, "then surely you can." At that, her eyes would sometimes flash in anger, her "how dare you tell me what I should do" look. But she didn't go away, and I could see her processing what I was saying.

I could also see that Maria was startled by her own success. "You did a great job," I said. "Oh?" she said. "Do you think so?"

And so Mary helped us begin what was to become a cycle of encouragement. We each saw the fear in the other, the hurt and the promise. We each pushed the other forward and, in so doing, began the great and wonderful process of freeing ourselves, moving toward the door that opened the way for love.

Chapter Four

I'll Wait, No Obligations

Over time, our friendship deepened. We were too shy with each other to ever say it, but we were soul mates and best friends, encouragers and supporters, cheerleaders and comrades-in-arms.

Time blurs for me with Maria, but we remained close friends for nearly two years. My marriage fell apart first, and I spent many hours with Maria in the studio barn, agonizing about my divorce, then plunging into that awful process. I did not even realize for a long time—and she never spoke of it—that her marriage was failing as well.

For almost a year, my wife and I were separated, and toward the end of that process, Maria filed for separation as well and began seeing her own therapist. We were not dating, I did not dare even broach the subject of our relationship, but then one day I was finally divorced. Maria was just a few months away. We had dinner or lunch together regularly, and I had begun ferrying popcorn, muffins, and tea into the studio barn. We talked for hours, about life, our work, my writing and my emerging sense of myself as a photographer, about dogs—especially her worries about Frieda. It was one of those rarest of relationships: we always had things to say, were always happy to see each other, always sad to say goodbye. Maria's sadness had deepened. She seemed to have no idea of what might become of her, what she would do, how she would survive or support herself.

The separation process had brought us nose to nose with reality. There was no place to hide.

I seemed to know that what I wanted was close, yet I was terrified at the thought of raising the subject—she might bolt.

There was an ethical question for me as well, a moral matter. We were both traumatized by our divorces. Everything I had heard and seen and read said it was not a good time to begin a new relationship.

I did not want to take advantage of her sadness or loneliness. I did not want to confuse her by declaring my love for her. Yet it was no longer honest or decent to hide it, or to hide from it.

The plan I conceived in my mind was this: I had to tell her how I felt. I had to point out our deepening closeness, to raise the issue of whether this was a healthy thing or not, whether we should simply keep away from each other for a while, until the dust cleared.

So one day, deep into our friendship, after we had both realized that our marriages were over, after we had both separated from our spouses and were about to be divorced, I went to the studio barn. I was terrified. I prayed and trembled and held my breath, then invited Maria onto the farmhouse porch. I said I needed to talk to her.

Of course, I could see from the look in her eyes that she understood that something serious was up. Knowing Maria, I guessed she was thinking that I would tell her that I had found someone. I later learned I was right.

While she put away the project she was working on, I made some tea and pulled two wicker chairs off to one side of the porch. I sat and waited for five or ten of the longest minutes of my life. Then I saw her exit the studio barn, walk up the driveway, open the gate, and come up onto the porch. She was smiling, but grimly, I thought. She was nervous, as was I.

I gathered all of the strength that I was aware of and much that I was not, and I told Maria that I thought I was developing "some feelings" for her. I added that it seemed that we each had "some feelings" for the other. Obviously, I said, it was an emotional time for both of us, so we shouldn't even think of doing anything about those feelings. We should wait. I knew she had to sort things out, and that she didn't want to plunge into another relationship. I understood that, I said. I did not want to put pressure on her. I wondered if what I was experiencing as I said those words was what a heart attack might feel like—shortness of breath, dizziness, pain in the chest.

What if she walked away? What if I scared her off?

I thought Maria would either slug me or bolt. She did neither. She just listened, and then she calmly got up and left.

I took it as good news that she didn't throw her tea in my face. Later, she said it was the bravest thing she had ever seen.

All she said to me that day was that she had to go home and walk Frieda.

Frieda, I thought. What about Frieda?

The next morning, I walked out to Maria's car while she was in the barn getting hay, and I pasted a yellow Post-it to the windshield.

"I'll wait. No obligations."

Maria read the note and never said a word about it, not then or later, other than the fact that she tore it up and ate it before she got home. "You ate it?" I asked her. "Yes," she said. She ate it. She never said why, and I have never asked her.

I have wondered sometimes if she knew how serious I was. That I would have waited, and would be waiting still, if she had driven away that day and not come back.

One evening, I got a call from the director of a dementia and Alzheimer's unit in a nearby nursing home. There was a riot in the facility, he said nervously. A food fight among the patients. "Could Izzy come?" he asked.

"Izzy? But he's a dog. Why don't you call the sheriff?"

"Because I don't want anybody to get arrested," he said.

Izzy and I roared off in my pickup. Sure enough, there was a nasty food fight going on.

I took Izzy off his lead and let him go. "Take care of it, boy," I said, like we were in the movies. I was that sure of him.

Izzy sailed up to the ringleader and put his nose on the man's knee. Soon everybody forgot that they were fighting, and they were all on the floor hugging and petting the dog. Izzy soaked it up. The cameras came out, and he began posing for the nurses and aides. They even took shots of Izzy for the nursing home's newsletter. He left with treats and biscuits.

When we got home, Izzy jumped out of the truck just as Maria was exiting the studio barn with Frieda. At the sight of Izzy walking off-leash up the driveway, Frieda went into a rage, roaring, lunging, almost pulling Maria off her feet. Izzy—poised, handsome, and cool as always—didn't even toss a glance Frieda's way. He acted as if she weren't there.

I hurried Izzy up the driveway and into the farmhouse.

Suddenly, I had a flash from my childhood. I remembered being in the fourth or fifth grade, staring in fury at the rich kids from my school who would not let me be on their team, who told me they would beat me up if I came near them or showed my face on the field. I hated their shiny shoes and slicked-back hair, despised their cocky and confident ways. I was furious, trembling with rage, nearly spitting in anger. I remember wanting to rush up the steps with a baseball bat and smash their teeth in.

Strange, I thought, that I should remember that day after so many years. But something clicked in me. I had never been very close to a dog like Frieda. But I am a person who, for one reason or another, has always lived outside of the circle, too.

I watched from a distance as the other kids played baseball, went to parties, fell in love. Later, it was bosses who made me feel low. Sometimes cocktail-party people. Or smug academics. Or pompous journalists. Or Ivy League types with connections. I have never moved much in literary circles or been welcome there. Some of this is them, some of it is me. I spent the first half of my life wanting to get inside the circle, the rest trying to stay out.

I thought I saw the scene before me from Frieda's perspective. Mine were beautiful, pampered dogs. Appropriate, well-behaved, featured on book covers all over the world. None of them (except for Izzy, who had lived a feral existence on a farm for years but who was quite unlike Frieda in that he was classically beautiful, well-bred, and quite content now) had ever missed a meal, had a tick for too long, skipped their shots, or gone a day without training, attention, or exercise. I thought she might have resented this. When I consider this interpretation, I have to laugh at myself. This was so much a reflection of me.

Frieda couldn't possibly have seen the story in this way. She had no idea what a book cover was, what it meant to be privileged; it was so much a human projection of a human's memory, a human's feelings. I was doing the very thing I so often urged people not to do—putting my story, my emotions, into the life of a dog. Whatever was going on with Frieda, it wasn't my history she was grappling with. I needed to understand hers.

As Frieda roared and growled and lunged, my dogs looked at her in astonishment, not able to comprehend what a dog like Frieda might be upset about. Only Rose, my other border collie, another dog who never surrendered, seemed to glower back, and even she never lost her composure the way Frieda did.

Still, I wondered what these dogs might look like to Frieda, who'd lived so far outside the circle, languishing month after month in a shelter. They must have appeared so alien to her. I was soon to learn much more about Frieda's history—her real story, not mine.

Maybe I could understand Frieda after all. Maybe I was even beginning to love her just a little bit.

Maria talked constantly about taking care of herself, living on her own, having time to breathe in her new life. She was deeply insecure about her own competence and her ability to get by without help. More than anything, she wanted to know that she could be responsible for herself.

Maria was not even sure she could rent an apartment on her own, but she did. She found a landlord who would accept Frieda—most would not—and rented a dingy two-room flat in a poor and run-down neighborhood of Granville, New York.

Granville is a shattered city about fifteen miles from my farm, and I had to bite my lip when I saw the tiny little outpost Maria and Frieda had moved into. I completely understood what Maria needed and wanted to do, but I know loneliness quite well, and this was a lonely and grim place, so different from the farm, so close and yet so far.

Granville was one of those hard-luck upstate New York communities: a once-prosperous mill town with its guts hollowed out by years of fleeing businesses and decline. The rumor about Granville was that it had more bars per capita than any other city in the United States. It looked that way.

I hated seeing Maria and Frieda holed up in this depressing apartment, but Maria did not see her new home that way. She saw it as beautiful, a place of her own, a step toward self-determination. That was something I needed to support. It would be an awful thing to undermine her in any way. I had to encourage her steps toward independence and the confidence that comes from leading your own life—something I needed to do as well. I had to be strong about that.

It was not really my business where Maria went. She didn't ask my opinion and I didn't offer one.

Maria had also worried that she wouldn't be able to find a job—there were not a lot of options in the remote rural area where we lived. She found a position as an aide and caretaker in a home for the emotionally disturbed. It was a tough job. It paid little, and the hours were erratic—two or three hours on weekday mornings and a twelve-hour shift on Sundays.

She took care of the residents in the home, helped feed and dress them, and drove them around to medical appointments and whatever entertainments they could afford—parks, bike rides, carnivals, and fairs. The residents were severely challenged and often difficult, sometimes violent. Before Maria started, a friend who knew both of us pulled me aside and urged me to tell Maria she shouldn't take the job. "She will never survive that," she told me.

I didn't agree. That advice was precisely the opposite of what I told Maria. "Of course you can do it," I said.

I worried sometimes that she might find the job depressing or too difficult. I was wrong. I kept my mouth shut, a new habit for me. Love can work miracles.

I could also see how good this job was for her—having her own money, her own place to go, doing work that was difficult but rewarding, that built confidence. There were lots of surprises and emergencies and conflicts in her job, and each day, as she handled every one, she seemed to grow stronger.

Maria was very clear on wanting some time alone, to build her confidence in caring for herself. She told me almost every day how many women there were out there in the world waiting for me, and how I should find one.

Chapter Five

The Dating Game (Sort Of)

The email came in just before midnight on a cold and snowy night.

Divorced in my sixth decade, getting a steady stream of AARP brochures and bombarded with ads for supplemental health insurance, I felt like I was supposed to spend the rest of my life alone until I got carted off to a nursing home.

Our culture is going through an especially cruel and greedy phase when it comes to aging. We older Americans are supposed to dry up, check our blood pressure, get our pills, replace worn-out parts, monitor our IRAs, and vanish. Love was not mentioned in any of the ads I was getting, and the doctors don't prescribe anything for it besides Viagra.

So I was especially grateful for different messages. The Internet often disconnects us from people. And then, in odd ways, it reconnects us.

"I have been struck by your writing on your blog," a woman wrote from out of the ether. "There is a loneliness, a sadness to your voice, I think. I believe I know where you are." She was sometimes sad and lonely, too.

A connection. I think being known is perhaps the most powerful element in love, something erectile dysfunction medicines don't provide. For so much of my life, I felt I was not known. I didn't know myself, and nobody knew me. Here, in the dark, through a wire, was somebody who said she did.

Email has been a part of my life for a couple of decades. In a former life I wrote for *Wired* and *Rolling Stone* magazines about technology, and I wrote for one of the first Internet blogs, *HotWired*. I get thousands of emails each week and am wary but generally confident about my ability to sense the nature of the person sending one. I know not to get personal with strangers. I know hostility is cheap and easy and doesn't count for much. But all that doesn't mean there aren't times when an unusual message pops up, one that touches me, engages me, gets me to pay attention.

This was such an email. It came from a woman studying to get her PhD at a midwestern university. She was a horticulturist and a writer. She studied plants, flowers, and weather. She also had a border collie and loved him very much, and, like me, she was recently divorced and living on a small farm. She sent me a link to her website, which was filled with beautiful photographs and stark, poignant writing about nature. This, I thought, might be a person I could live with, talk to, share my life with.

I had made some terrible mistakes in my former marriage, and one of them was living a separate life. That would not happen again. If I was going to be alone, then so be it, but I wouldn't pretend I was with someone if I wasn't.

In many ways, this woman was just what I wanted. Creative, articulate, thoughtful, in touch with the world of nature and animals, sensitive, encouraging . . .

Like Maria, I thought.

I looked out the farmhouse window and over at the studio barn. I saw that the lights were on, and that Maria's ugly little Toyota Yaris (I called it her toilet bowl with wheels) was parked across the street.

When I gave Maria the use of the studio barn, its ownership changed. It no longer felt like mine. Nor did I feel comfortable going into it without her permission. If we started visiting each other in the night, that would be a whole other story, so I never did.

But this night, rereading this special email, I was excited. I thought of responding to this woman, perhaps even visiting her farm or asking her to come here. We had so much in common.

On an impulse, I got up, put my boots on, and walked across the street, making as much noise as I could so as not to startle Maria. I had microwaved some popcorn. I had noticed how gaunt Maria seemed, and although she always said she wasn't hungry, she would devour the bread and cheese and fruit and tea I brought her, as if she hadn't eaten for a week. If I asked her if she wanted anything, she would say no, so I stopped asking and just brought it. She always ate it, every bit.

I wanted to share this email with her, but I also thought she might like the popcorn. Maybe it would give her some energy while she worked. As I approached the door I heard Frieda's roar—Maria brought her late at night, sometimes, for safety—and I heard Maria rushing her into the crate, where she would stare at me and growl for as long as I was there.

I came to the side door and tapped. Maria appeared in the window.

She saw I was holding the popcorn. "You didn't need to do that," she said. She smiled. "Come in," she said. I apologized for interrupting her. I felt strange being there so late at night.

It was her place now, not mine, and if I wanted her to be comfortable there, I had to think of it that way. She had brought in overstuffed chairs, piles of quilts and fabrics, a teapot she plugged into the wall, and a chalkboard on which she wrote poems, ideas, thoughts. Incense filled the space with a sweet smell. The studio barn had been transformed, from a run-down old shed into a warm, creative place. Maria had brought this ugly little barn magically to life.

If Maria and I felt like soul mates in our friendship, there were plenty of ways in which we could not have been more different. Like when it came to money. When I bought Bedlam Farm, I raided antiques barns and furniture stores for months, filling up my new home with expensive furniture, hiring a platoon of workers to do the floors, windows, and walls.

Maria does not hire people to do things and rarely, if ever, sets foot in a retail store. Watching her redo the studio barn shocked and shamed me. She made curtains out of old sheets and other fabrics, found stuffed chairs at yard sales and on front lawns (with "Free" signs on them), painted the walls, and built shelves. Candles flickered in the night, and odd chants wafted from an old CD player.

I never saw her bring anything into the barn, or witnessed her doing this restoration. She flitted about like a genie, and the barn was simply transformed into an artist's studio, stones and feathers on the windowsills, fabrics sorted out in boxes and on shelves. She had a bucket of water for Frieda and biscuits in a bowl.

This is what Maria does. She doesn't even see ugly or angry. She looks at Frieda and perceives an adorable and beautiful spirit. She steps into a neglected and ungainly little "barn" and imagines it as an enchanting workplace. She looks at a rag and visualizes a beautiful quilt. Most of what I needed I ordered from L. L. Bean. Would she look at crazy, battered me and see a soul mate? This is one of the things I have always loved about Maria. She recognizes the best parts of a thing and transforms the whole into something beautiful.

Maria had come to the door right away, almost as if she had been expecting me. This might have been a projection, I feared. But I always had the sense that while she was happy in the studio barn, she was also lonely, not so much for me but for something more than she had. There was a piercing aloneness about her that almost never went away. She seemed to drift around the edges of things, going through the motions, but she never seemed to cross over, to join in. I didn't know where this sense of loneliness came from, only that it was there.

I said that I was sorry to bother her but I had to show her something. She smiled. We both sat down, munching our popcorn, while Maria read the email I had printed out.

"Nice," she said.

I smiled. This was great.

"Did you see how old she is?" Maria asked me, grinning.

No, I hadn't.

"She's twenty-six," she said. "Tear it up and don't answer it."

Maria laughed. The air seeped out of my balloon. Lord, twenty-six. What was wrong with me? And thus we added a new routine to our repertoire. I played the cute but clueless older man seeking love, and Maria was the wise, young female pal rolling her eyes and protecting him, giving him advice, instructing him in the wily ways of women.

"It's the book tour you have to watch out for," she kept telling me. "They'll see that you don't have a ring. The women will all come after you." Lots of people were telling me that, and it was unnerving. I have never thought of myself as attractive in any way. The fact that Maria seemed to see me this way shocked me, and perhaps excited me as well.

I had been hiding out on my farm—my therapist called it "Fort Bedlam"—for some years now, writing my books, taking my photos, sailing out once a year on a long book tour, only to return to my remote lair, immerse myself in farm chores, and brood. If you are looking to avoid intimacy, I can show you how. I did it for years.

But now it was true. I was officially dating. I was out there. I did not see myself as a hot opportunity, but things did begin to happen. I went to a nearby clinic to get an infected foot injury treated. The doctor was nice; she recognized me and we chatted about dogs, country life, and people we both knew.

She asked me about my life, and if I was under stress, and I told her about my divorce. I returned home with my antibiotics, and several hours later, the dogs barked as a car pulled into the driveway.

I was surprised to see the doctor from the clinic. She was carrying a large tray with tinfoil over it.

"I brought you some lasagna," she said, "in case you didn't have anything for dinner." Too stunned to say much, I mumbled my thanks, and she left. I was terrified. Doctors won't come to your house if you're dying, let alone to bring you dinner. When I told Maria about this gift, she laughed. "You don't get it, do you? She was approaching you, seeing if you were interested." This was hard for me to believe. But apparently it was true.

When I thought of the woman I wanted to be with, no single image came to mind. I had gotten only this far: I wanted to be with someone who wanted to share my life. A creative person. A person who would encourage me and create things on her own. A gentle and loving person, someone who loved rural life as much as I did, and who was drawn to the life of animals.

One day, I went to a hospice funeral and was enchanted by a beautiful undertaker who reached into the top of her dress, pulled out a harmonica, and then belted out a dynamite rendition of "Amazing Grace," nearly elbowing the minister off the podium. She was wild, alluring, different.

She loved sheep, she told me (she knew I had some), and

asked if she could come over and dissect one if he or she died. I have to say, she got me all flustered. A beautiful undertaker? Dissecting sheep on the farm? And she does a great "Amazing Grace"? Now, that sounded promising.

I brought news of this exotic find to Maria. She gave me that wry smile of hers and asked me if the undertaker had had a wedding ring on her finger. I said I hadn't noticed. A few weeks later, I ran into my undertaker friend and her husband at a diner in Fort Edward. Maria suggested that I might not be quite ready for dating. (I didn't tell her that the beautiful undertaker couldn't have been more than twenty-five.)

I started to realize that Maria thought I was kind of cute, funny, and endearing. Once I got wind of that, I played to it, bringing her stories of my women, so that she would find me cuter, more endearing, give me more of those fabulous smiles.

In Saratoga Springs, I met a woman at the supermarket; she was standing behind me in the checkout line. She was in her mid-fifties, with her hair back in a bun, and had a craggy, handsome face. She looked like an artist, and we both recognized that quality in each other. We got to talking, and she said I seemed familiar; it turned out she recognized my voice from a series of local NPR broadcasts on dogs I had done.

The line got jammed up by some computer issue, and I was startled when she offered me a drink (from the case of cold sodas and bottled water near the register). We talked as we checked out and continued our conversation in front of the store. I learned that she was a poet who taught at a nearby liberal arts college. I liked her gentle manner. She had also gotten divorced recently, and had also moved to the country from the

New York City area. She had two yellow Labs she loved dearly and hiked with every day in the parks and trails outside Saratoga.

Her "country" was different from mine. Saratoga is a booming, wealthy city, a far cry from the tiny, gritty town where I live. She talked about how much she loved teaching and poetry. A fantasy of the Saratoga-Hebron life flashed through my mind: Labs. Poetry. Good restaurants and bookstores punctuated by the quiet life of the farm. A creative life filled with books and art.

She said she was a photographer and painted watercolors. We joked about the teenaged cashiers and about forgetting things and other age-related annoyances. She had an easy laugh. How nice it was to talk to somebody who knew about getting older, when your feet and knees always seemed to hurt and it was hard not to fear what lay not too far ahead.

But then I hesitated. This couldn't work. What about Maria? She had just settled into the studio barn, and would surely bolt or be uncomfortable if another person turned up on the farm. Knowing her, I understood that she would not presume to force her presence on a new person, a new woman. She might simply vanish in the night, just as she so often came and went in the night. I couldn't bear that.

The poet and I exchanged cards and said goodbye. Some weeks later, I got a lovely email from her:

"Jon, I haven't heard from you, so I can safely assume it wasn't in the cards for us to get to know each other better. Too bad, I would have liked that, but I understand. I wish you well and I hope our paths cross." Every now and then, I go to her website to look at her photography and watercolors. I see she has published a new volume of poetry. I hope she has found someone.

It was one of the nicest times I have ever had in a supermarket.

The encounters with women continued. A reporter interviewed me over dinner in Saratoga, but after dinner, it seemed we were not doing business anymore. She asked me if I was ever lonely. If I might want to go hiking in Vermont.

This terrified me, and I said no.

At a book signing in Cincinnati, a woman came up to me and introduced herself. "Look," she said, "I'm looking to make a change in my life, and I can tell from your blog that you are divorced, and I see you have no ring. Forgive me, but I'd love to come share your life on Bedlam Farm, if we got to know each other." She was an architect, she said, and she was lonely and sick of dating. She loved the idea of life on the farm. If I wasn't interested, that was fine. She was just asking.

I said I was flattered and appreciated her honesty—and I did—but I wasn't ready to try something like that. She thanked me, shook my hand, and left. I never saw her or heard from her again.

A woman gave me a note tucked inside a book; it asked if she could visit me at my hotel after the signing. I fled to the men's room and hid there.

A woman came up to me while I was having breakfast at a hotel in Seattle and asked if she could join me. She overwhelmed me by going on and on about how much she loved my work. I got up and left and ordered room service.

So it was true. There were lonely people out there. They were interested in me. But for some reason, I was not interested in them. Not a one.

Complicating matters was the fact that I was trying to negotiate all this under the influence of a full-blown nervous breakdown. I felt myself physically and emotionally disintegrating.

In Austin, before speaking at the Texas Book Festival, I came undone, lying on the bathroom floor of my hotel room, vomiting and shaking. It was Halloween, and I ended up walking the streets of that fascinating city most of the night. My media escort, Lucy, was a friendly, sympathetic woman, and I opened up to her about my divorce at dinner. The next day she called and said she had a friend she wanted me to meet. From our talk, she thought we might enjoy each other.

At five, I met Lucy on the veranda of a downtown Austin hotel for drinks. The street was clogged with University of Texas students and government workers. Suddenly, a tall, beautiful woman with long brown hair and two Canon cameras—one slung over the right shoulder, one slung over the left—appeared in front of me. She introduced herself as Donna, a university photographer and an admirer of my books.

I was slack-jawed. I had never seen anyone like Donna, a camera commando with great gear. In addition to the two top-of-the-line Canons, she had two lens holsters slung over each hip, like six-shooters in a Western.

"Hey," she said, offering her hand. "I hear you're a photographer! Let's go take some pictures." I grabbed my Canon camera, and we went outside. She had an unorthodox style. If she saw a subject she liked, she walked up to him or her, pointed to the camera, and said, "Hey there, I'm going to take your photo" in a voice that did not seem to contemplate hesitation or disagreement.

She whipped out a disk, stuck it into a portable player she pulled out of her pocket, and showed me some beautiful portraits of students and people on the street.

Was this a date? How could I possibly keep up with this woman? I was overwhelmed. Donna was beautiful, charismatic, and fun. Was I supposed to like her? I thought of Maria: quiet, artistic, gentle. So soft-spoken and low-key, so unlike this woman, who seemed to want to get to know me.

After taking some photos on the street, Donna and I returned to sit with Lucy and have a drink. Donna offered a sharp and useful critique of my photography, gave me good ideas about light and centering, then abruptly stood up and said she had to go back to work. Was I up for breakfast at six the next morning? "We could head out to the university or even the Hill Country beyond and do some early morning shooting, in the good light. Think about it," she said. "I'll email you in an hour or two." And then she was gone.

Lucy looked at me, smiling as she called for the bill. "She's something, isn't she?" And then she left.

I grabbed my cell and called Maria. I told her about Donna.

"She sounds exciting," she said. "What do you think?"

"I don't want to have breakfast with her. Am I crazy? If we got together, she'd be sitting around holding towels in the room while I threw up." Yes, Maria said, I probably was crazy. But that didn't mean I had to have breakfast with Donna. I agreed.

Besides, I thought, she was a bit intense. Although I made a note to check into those lens hip holsters. In fact, I went online as soon as I had a chance, to find some.

What did I want, I wondered. Somebody I could talk to as easily as Maria.

The book tour was an interesting time. In Dayton, a young woman said she would happily move to Bedlam Farm to live with me and my dogs, and once she had installed herself there, we could see if things might go further. A woman in Portland said she felt my energy through my blog, and did I want to go out for some coffee or tea?

Women brought me gifts—biscuits, handkerchiefs, books, photographs, knitted socks and gloves. It was hard to separate enthusiastic fans from women who were interested in a relationship. And I didn't want to presume that people who were just talking to me had any ulterior motives.

I was not prepared to discuss my divorce with strangers, and I didn't. But a lot of people wanted to discuss it with me. And what was I expecting? I had written five memoirs. I wrote a blog about my life. I was interviewed about my work all over the country. Did I think people wouldn't notice what was going on?

Still, when I returned from the book tour, I had not made a single connection I wanted to pursue. Nor had I had a single date. This was something I was going to discuss with my romantic adviser. If the book tour wasn't going to work, then where would I meet a potential partner?

While my friendship with Maria deepened, another friendship began to evolve, this one between Frieda and Lenore, the dog I'd gotten at roughly the same time Maria had adopted Frieda. The dog I called the Hound of Love. The dog I slept with on winter nights and, uncharacteristically, sang lullabies and love songs to.

My therapist, a steely-eyed and unsparing truth teller, said, "Don't you see? Lenore is what you want in a human being. It's coming out that way, as it often does with dogs."

I was shocked by this insight, surprisingly. Hadn't I written books on just this subject? Hadn't I studied this very phenomenon—humans projecting their feelings and desires onto companion animals? And yet I didn't see it when it was happening to me.

One afternoon, Lenore was coming down the driveway with me and ran smack into Frieda, who was on a leash with Maria.

Lenore was about three years old then and still puppyish. She is a boundlessly affectionate dog, in the way Labs can sometimes be, and doesn't seem to even comprehend the idea of rejection or aggression. She had charmed two donkeys, a ram, two barn cats, and even my serious sheepherding dog, Rose, in her time on the farm. But I was terrified of what Frieda might do to a creature as loving and trusting as this. And I was about to find out.

When Frieda saw Lenore, she roared and lunged forward,

pulling Maria up the hill. A gentle soul, Maria is usually as astonished by aggression as Lenore is, and she has the same reaction: she freezes. Suddenly, Lenore and Frieda were nose to nose.

Lenore dropped to the ground, tail wagging, while Frieda, rigid and menacing, stood right over her, growling. Judging from Frieda's stance, she was ready to fight.

Maria was trying to pull her back, but she wouldn't move, and Frieda is not an easy dog to move when she doesn't want to. I knew the best thing to do was nothing, so I just stood stock-still. Any lunging or interference could just make things worse. It is a difficult thing to do, watching while your dog is in a vulnerable position, but it is the best thing to do.

From her nearly prone position on the ground, Lenore lifted her chin up and licked Frieda on the nose. Then, as Frieda blinked in surprise, Lenore licked her on the nose again. Lenore is a warrior for love, and she simply does not comprehend or accept rejection. Her greatest defense, I think, is that she has no conception of defense.

Frieda looked confused.

Then something changed in Frieda. She relaxed her stance, lowered her head, and sniffed Lenore carefully around her nose and neck, Lenore's tail wagging like the rotor blade on a helicopter the whole time.

After a minute, Lenore got up and stood next to Frieda, and I suggested that we all walk together on the path. Frieda seemed to accept Lenore, was calmer around her. We walked along with no trouble, and I learned some things from that encounter.

Frieda was not an aggressive dog. She was constantly asserting her dominance, seeking control, feeling as if she had to do something. But if she had really wanted to harm Lenore, it would have been easy enough to accomplish.

I also saw that Lenore had worked a bit of her magic on Frieda. She had calmed her down, settled her, grounded her in some way I had not seen before.

But mostly, I was just glad Frieda had not eaten Lenore.

Chapter Six

Me and Davy Crockett at the Alamo

On tour, away from the farm, out of my fortress, I was disintegrating rapidly. One time, I had a panic attack on a plane and it was so severe that I had to get off at a connecting stop. Normally very comfortable with public speaking, I started breaking out in a cold sweat when I entered a bookstore. I couldn't eat, sleep, or quiet my mind. As I've said, in Austin I found myself lying on the bathroom floor of a hotel room at three o'clock in the morning, sweating, shaking, sick to my stomach.

I called Maria often—I had asked her to watch over the animals while I was gone, and suddenly alone on the farm in midautumn, she was having a difficult time as well—and she helped me relax and breathe. If she had not picked up the phone, I would have called an ambulance. That's how bad it was. It was Halloween, and I could hear the sounds of a parade—singing, honking, cheering. I was lying on the white tile floor of an Austin hotel room, naked, weeping and throwing up into the toilet bowl. When I could speak, I called Maria. "Just breathe," she said. "Breathe with me." And we did: we breathed together, even across the country, completely in sync, crawling back to life together, so close, so accepting, so present.

As sick as I was, I had a revelation that night. I knew that Maria and I were meant to be more to each other than just buddies. If she could sit by the phone for an hour at three A.M., listening to me crying and so desperate for her help, if she could accept that and be there for me as long as I needed her, then we were destined to be together, even if it would take a while, even if it wouldn't happen quite the way I wanted it to.

Frieda was the elephant in the room, looming larger in my mind.

For one thing, I was still afraid of her, as was almost everyone who met her, except Maria. I thought that if I pushed her too hard, she would come after me. And then we would have a much more fraught problem to solve. She was a one-person dog, powerfully bound to Maria, and I had a lot of other issues going on in my life. Training a dog like Frieda requires calmness, patience, courage, and clarity, and those were in short supply in my life at the time.

I wanted Maria to move in with me before she changed her mind and saw what a mess I was. Everyone I knew, including Maria, thought I was moving way too fast. I'm impulsive; it's just the way I am. She didn't pay much attention to it, then or now.

But I couldn't ask her to give up Frieda, and I was not sure she would have had I asked. And I couldn't bring Frieda into the farm without jeopardizing my dogs and the other farm animals. I had been through a brutal ordeal with my dog Orson, whom I'd been unable to train or cure or calm. My refusal to accept that some dogs are simply beyond our reach cost him dearly. One of the options I considered with Orson after he attacked a child and bit him on the neck was confining him, building a secure kennel and making sure he spent the rest of his life in it. This was the solution many people felt I should have pursued. I didn't because I knew this arousable and loyal creature would hate such confinement, and would fight being kept apart from and out of so much of my life. I have never considered confining a dog for life to be a humane solution. It might make us feel better, but it is not in any way a natural life for a dog.

And I was facing the same situation with Frieda. The only way I could see her being on the farm was to build a secure kennel and keep her in it. No walks in the woods, no visits to the house, no participation in our lives, which is the thing I most value about having a dog. And then, still, there would be the one time we got lazy, distracted, or confused, and some kid on a bike or motorcycle driver or deliveryman would pay. It felt frighteningly familiar to me.

I had to find a better solution. Because by then I knew I loved Maria more than anything in the world, and what got me up off that bathroom floor that night and back to work was the thought that she would be waiting for me at the airport.

I've read it so often that it seems a cliché to me, but love is, in fact, the greatest healer. It saved my life. I was taking on a lifetime's worth of change, and it was daunting, but I had never had a stronger or more powerful motivation for being strong, getting well, moving ahead with my life.

When I felt the terror sweeping through my body like a poison, I had the most powerful and healing antidote in the world: I would imagine Maria, see her smile, feel her touch, her kiss on my forehead as she said, "And how is my handsome man today?"

She had said this strange thing to me once or twice, while holding my hand. We were beginning to touch; our goodbye hugs were getting longer, closer, more meaningful.

At first, when I heard those words, I was astonished, uneasy. I had never heard such words before; they could not be true, not about me. And when I felt myself falling off that steep cliff, I would close my eyes and think of that handsome man, and I would step back off the edge.

Once when Maria said I was handsome, I said she must be crazy, and I saw the hurt and anger in her eyes. I thought of a better response the next time she said it. I said thank you, and thought of the small miracles in a world where a woman like that would say this to a man like me.

It was a hot day in San Antonio. I had not slept in three nights and was sick to my stomach. In a few hours, I would be speaking to one thousand people. I was sweating, and my hands were shaking. My stomach felt as if someone had stuck an ice pick in it. I did not know what to do.

I had been on the phone with Maria all night, and I didn't want to call her again.

My media escort was worried. She kept asking me if I was okay, if I needed to see a doctor. The day before, in Austin, I had gone AWOL during a Texas Book Festival reception for authors at the LBJ Presidential Library. My publicist back in New York had nearly called the police to find me. Cellphones had been ringing everywhere, including in my pocket.

The idea that sent me AWOL had come into my head as I was pushing the panic away. I'd wanted to make the relationship real. I'd wanted it to be a part of my body—to get a tattoo for her. If I had called Maria and asked her about it, she would have laughed, perhaps been horrified, told me not to do it. It was too soon. We weren't even living together. At the same time, I also knew that a part of her would be pleased at this over-the-top declaration of love. Like me, Maria didn't feel worthy of love, entitled to it. Like me, she was a romantic, a sucker for romantic gestures. She also had this powerful sense of honor about our relationship. In her mind, it was okay to hang out, to go on dates, to talk to each other all day, but not to go further, to sleep together or live together. Not until she was officially divorced, which was some months away. She didn't want to hurt anyone.

I had a different view of it, perhaps because my ex-wife and family were living hours away. My marriage was over; we were simply negotiating the details. And I was older. I wanted to experience true love before I went on Social Security.

Sometimes in life you have to be cautious. Sometimes you have to put caution aside and follow your heart, and it is never really clear when you should do one or the other. Maria always understood that about me, that I needed to move quickly.

I knew I was way ahead of the relationship—putting somebody's name on your body is a big leap forward when you haven't even had sex together. But it was my way of showing my love, of persuading her, and I knew on some instinctive level that she would love it, or at least admire it. It was my equivalent of crossing the castle moat to serenade the princess under the window, even though it could result in my head getting chopped off. A romantic gesture, a manifestation of great love. It was a risk, but worth it. I asked my media escort to drive me to a tattoo parlor. She was convinced she'd be fired for taking me to get a tattoo while the library officials were waiting for me, but I can be very persuasive.

And we had connected with each other. Her son had been grievously injured in a car crash, and she understood, as I did, the importance of making days count.

"Does she love you?" asked Carlotta, the eighteen-year-old receptionist at the tattoo parlor. "Are you sure? It's a big step." This teenager, with her nose, chin, and ears pierced, seemed like a mystic to me, a wise woman closer to romance than I had been. I said I wanted something a bit fierce—like a skull and crossbones—but Jamie, the parlor manager, an artist studying at the University of Texas, vetoed that. It better be something your girlfriend likes, he said. Like a flower.

I told Carlotta about Maria, about our lives, about calling her at three A.M. from the hotel bathroom and how she'd breathed with me for an hour. How we were both getting divorced, were both terrified. How we weren't quite a couple yet but were so close.

"Okay, she loves you," she said. "Get the tattoo." I called Maria from the tattoo parlor—the escort had given up and gone to get some food for me—and I asked Maria what her favorite flower was but wouldn't say why I was asking.

She laughed. "Okay, a daisy," she said, and I knew she knew. From the first, we always knew what was in each other's head. And when I got home and showed her the tattoo, she laughed, and said, "You're crazy to do that. We just started dating. You shouldn't have done it. And I love you for it." And she did.

I knew that Maria was starved for love, as was I—and I also needed to show her how much I loved her. We had lived much of our lives without love, and I believed neither of us would let it go. Besides, Carlotta told me, I could always cover the daisy with a snake or a sword if things didn't work out.

But Maria and I were already a couple in some of the most important ways. Maria saw through the fear, the panic, the vomiting and shaking, into the soul of the person underneath, the real me. She never really saw me as the person I was on the floor of that bathroom. She never paid much attention to that version of me, as if it were a mood that would soon pass.

I knew we would be together, one way or another, one day, and for good. The rest was just space to cross. She had to heal, and she had to be loved. But the tattoo was a powerful message—*I love you enough to put your name on my body*—and she got it.

I finally made it to the LBJ library in Austin that day, my shirt oozing blood and ink from the tattoo. That night, I flew to San Antonio. When I tried to pay for checking my bags, my credit card was refused. (I had purchased camera equipment minutes before, and American Express had decided that I might be a thief.)

On the plane to San Antonio, I thought more about Frieda. I was starting to obsess about her. It was a huge bump in the road to sharing our lives together. Maria loved Frieda dearly, and I couldn't ask her to leave Frieda behind; nor was I certain that she would. And Frieda could not be with my dogs or the other animals on the farm. What would I do? How would we resolve this? Maria adored Frieda and saw her as a surrogate child. Frieda had been through plenty. Could I subject her to another rehoming, and if so, who would take her?

And what would it do to my relationship with Maria if I asked her to give up Frieda, or if I were confronted with such a choice?

That was not the way I wanted to start our relationship; it was not my idea of love or trust or commitment. I wouldn't put her in that situation.

Bringing Frieda back to a shelter was not an option. Given that the dog had languished in one for nearly a year, it was unlikely that she would be adopted.

And there was no reason to think about euthanizing her. She was a healthy dog, and she had not yet bitten anybody or done serious harm, although not for want of trying.

She deserved a second chance too, and she loved Maria as much as I did. And there was no greater gift I could give Maria than for Frieda to be able to live with us.

As soon as the hot Texas sun came up, I left the hotel in San Antonio. I'd woken at two A.M., shaking, running to the bathroom, ill, and had then stared at the ceiling for a few hours before deciding I needed to get out and collect myself if I were to have any chance of giving my next speech. I started walking around the downtown; I wandered around that beautiful city's old streets for nearly an hour, not sure where I was going, until I came to an old adobe building that seemed very familiar. But I had to look at the plaques and signs before I realized where I was.

I was standing in front of the Alamo.

Like many boomer kids, I'd grown up with Walt Disney's version of American history, and Davy Crockett and the story of the Alamo had loomed very large in my life.

I'd watched Fess Parker as Crockett every week as a child, mesmerized by the story of this brave frontiersman willing to give his life for a cause he believed in. I had a coonskin cap and a frontier rifle. I went to sleep a thousand times imagining Crockett's last stand. I hated the Mexican general Santa Anna for the brutal way he'd massacred the Alamo defenders, and I wondered at the courage and dedication of the small band who'd defended this little mission. Would I ever have that kind of courage? Could I be that brave?

And standing there looking at it, I felt all those feelings come rushing back. I was shocked at how unimposing the Alamo actually was, and I could hardly imagine how Crockett and the Texans had stood their ground against a large Mexican army.

Like an awestruck schoolkid, I stood at the gate and peered in. The building was beautiful, spare, and the grounds meticulously well tended.

It was two hours before opening time. An elderly guard smiled at me through the closed entry. "So this is the Alamo," I said.

I started talking with the guard, who was happy to explain the history of the Alamo and Texas's battle for independence.

Suddenly, he looked at his watch, opened the gate, and waved me in. Then he walked me to the far side of the graceful mission house—much less dramatic than I had imagined it—and pointed to the steps leading up to the second floor.

"It was up there," he said. "We believe Davy Crockett died right up there, standing off a bayonet charge by about a hundred soldiers."

I've been to Gettysburg, the Washington and Lincoln monuments, the Tomb of the Unknown Soldier. I was moved by all of them. But standing where Davy Crockett made his last stand, I was nearly speechless.

The guard told me I had five minutes—he had to make some rounds—and I turned and looked up at the searing Texas sun.

I don't know to this day if I merely conjured it, but I felt a rush of air and saw a burst of light, and there he was: Davy Crockett, in his coonskin cap, with his rifle in his arms and blood on his leather shirt.

"Hey," I said, thinking I had just pushed past sleep deprivation and panic, into something stranger.

"Hey," he said. "You know what?"

"What?" I said.

"You're a pussy, Jon Katz."

"What?" I asked, incredulous. Davy Crockett, right here, talking to me, calling me a pussy?

"Yep," he said. "You're a pussy. I got shot here along with a bunch of good people defending an idea, and you are falling apart over a divorce and a dog. You should be ashamed of yourself."

"But, sir . . ." I heard myself stammering.

"Nothing much to say," he told me. "Get focused, snap out of it. Go and give your speech and get home and take care of things. This is no place to whine or fall apart."

And then he vanished. Crockett may have been a projection of what I wished I was feeling, a vision of the courage I wished I had. I have often told this story as a kind of joke, a reflection of my neediness and silliness. Some stories grow and deepen over time, though, and I don't tell it as a joke any longer.

The subconscious is a powerful, if underappreciated, thing. Texas sure stirred mine up. I knew I could not survive living with that level of fear. I could not write my books, live on my farm, take my photos, be a good lover and friend to Maria. David Crockett was a radiant seed of memory for me, buried deep in my consciousness, emerging when I was desperate to find my strength, a way through my Alamo. Crockett saw the fear that had lived inside me for so long.

I'm not sure I will ever understand why I listened to this ghost, this figment of my imagination. Standing in the Alamo brought me back to the formation of me, and Crockett saw me more clearly than I saw myself. Of course I would survive the divorce. Of course I could get through it. People stood on parapets and gave their lives for causes I could barely understand.

People died from disease, violence, war; they were hit by cars, felled by cancer. Practically everyone I knew had gotten divorced, and I had made my decision willingly, set out on a search for love, and had found it, against all odds, right across the street. Even there, at the Alamo, I knew I was speaking not to Davy Crockett but to myself.

If he could give his life on that battlement, I could move ahead with mine.

I took out my cellphone and called Maria. I woke her up.

"Maria, you won't believe this," I said. "Davy Crockett just chewed me out—he called me a pussy."

"You're right," she said, "I don't believe it." I explained to her that I was at the Alamo and had run into Davy Crockett. He had given me great advice: apparently, I was going to give my speech and go home.

"That sounds good," Maria said, trying to keep the skepticism out of her voice. "Maybe you want to get something to eat . . ."

That, of course, was one of the many things I loved about Maria. Many people would have rolled their eyes and hung up, started looking for a sane person, but Maria never turned away from me, never found me too much, too strange, too crazy.

Her skepticism didn't matter. I listened to Davy Crockett. I believed he was telling me something I needed to hear. Divorce was painful, and I was frightened. But people had survived worse and sacrificed themselves for much more. So would I.

I felt better, stronger, inspired.

My tattoo was an affirmation, not only of Maria but of the strength I needed to get my life back. It was a statement to the world: I was strong, I was in love, I was not afraid of it.

For my generation, heroes were simpler, more black-and-white. We never knew what they were really like, only what they told us. Succeeding generations are not so lucky. In the information age, with the death of privacy, the erosion of space, heroes do not last much longer than lunch. My heroes were honest and brave, and they were not pussies. They inspired me. Death did not faze them, let alone divorce and change. And they always got the girl.

When I charged into the convention center that day, the thousand-plus crowd that stared back at me didn't faze me a bit. I gave a good speech, and I was grateful that I didn't wuss out a stone's throw from Crockett's last stand, and then later, on the airplane home, I resolved to be worthy of David Crockett and make him proud. One day I'd go back to the Alamo—perhaps with the girl—and he would tell me so.

If he could stand off hundreds of soldiers for days, I could train a dog to live in my life. And get the girl, too.

Chapter Seven

Frieda's War

"Rose, let's get to work," I shouted, heading out the side door. I didn't know that Maria was about to walk with Frieda on the path into the woods, that they were heading to the driveway where Rose was working. The very sight of Rose always seemed to challenge Frieda in the most basic and primal way.

I was still hoping that one day soon Frieda would get comfortable enough to come and live on the farm and share my life there. Maria, too.

Sometimes, Maria would come by the farm to walk up my hill and on the path into the woods that adjoined the farm, and that was where she and Frieda were heading when they ran into Rose that day, not long after I'd returned from my book tour.

Rose was at the bottom of the driveway, near the road, where she knew to wait for me, and I was about ten feet behind her. I saw her go stiff, and her ears go down, and then, a moment later, I saw this brown-and-black blur come charging out from behind the fence right at her.

I had no time to think, but I moved quickly. Rose had never backed down from any confrontation. She had herded sheep, battled rams, brawled with wild pigs, stood down coyotes. She simply didn't have a retreat mode. How else could you control thousands of pounds of livestock if you weighed only thirty-seven pounds? But although she was tough, she was not a fighter. Border collies are slight; they have short, narrow teeth, good for nipping a balky ewe but not for fighting rottweiler-shepherd mixes with their powerful jaws, large teeth, and much greater body weight. Frieda was a fighting and hunting machine, and she threw her body into Rose, knocking her over as Rose barked and snapped. It was nothing like an even match, and I had a terrifying image of Frieda getting Rose by the throat and hurting, maybe killing her.

Dog fights seem to go on for a long time, but they rarely do, and I was on the two animals in a second, lashing out with my sneakered foot, catching Frieda on her right side as I heard Rose yelp out in pain and surprise. Rose had never seen an animal quite like this one.

My foot barely grazed Frieda, and I was half-expecting her to bite it off, but she didn't. She surprised me. She looked at me for what seemed the longest time, as if in surprise. And then she just lay down.

I yelled at Rose to back off and checked for blood; there was none.

I sent Rose across the road and turned back to Frieda, who was still lying down looking at me, emitting a low growl.

Maria was standing in the road, her eyes wide, a look of horror and fright on her face. I knew what had happened. Frieda had spotted Rose and popped the leash right out of Maria's hand.

I've always come from an unorthodox place in terms of thinking about dogs. And lots of my ideas have gotten me into trouble. I believe dogs who harm people ought to leave this world. I believe it is noble to find a better home for your dog if you can and if a change is appropriate. I believe most dog-training books are not very useful. I do not believe that dogs have souls. Or that many suffer from separation anxiety. Or that they are children, or communicate and think like human beings. Or that locking them in crates for their whole lives so human beings can feel better about themselves is humane. Nor do I believe that they cure depression, sniff out chronic illness, foretell death, or let us know when they are ready to die.

I do not wish to meet all of my dogs at the end of that bridge, either, so that they can chase balls for me for all eternity. I want more for them than that, and I hope they find it.

Dogs are amazing and wonderful creatures. They give us great unconditional love and meaningful companionship; they make us feel better, soothe the ill and infirm, open us up, connect us to the outside world. But I believe perspective is important and that many people who love dogs are in danger of losing it.

I have learned some things in the decade or so since I began writing about dogs, and I expect and hope to learn much more. Mostly, I think we know much less about these remarkable creatures than we think we do, and we are still struggling for a language and a consciousness that might help us understand them.

The challenge for me, from the beginning, was to find a way to talk to Frieda. I wanted to talk to her with my heart and soul, not just my mouth. Training is a spiritual experience for me, not about obedience but about communication and trust.

I love my dogs more than I can say, and they have opened up my life in more ways than I can relate. As I have opened up as a human being, and have learned to listen to and accept them as the wonderful animals they are, my relationships with them have deepened. Lenore showed me how to love when I was love-less. Izzy brought me to the transforming experience of helping people leave the world. Rose helped give me the strength to live my life in the country on my farm. Frieda was bringing me to Maria in ways I did not yet understand.

Every dog I have lived with has made me a better human— more patient, less distracted, a better listener. And Frieda was no exception. In fact, she may have opened up my life more than all of the other dogs put together, although she surely came at it from a very different place, and in a very new and different way.

Frieda was, I think, a dog at war with the world. And I was a person at war with the world. The one thing we really shared was a great love for Maria. Looking back, I think that this love, more than anything else, connected us, and motivated us to stick it out with each other. Maria would have been heartbroken if she had had to choose between us, and neither of us would have ever wanted to do anything to harm Maria.

At the same time, I threatened Frieda's view of the world, and her grip on Maria. Maria was now drawn to someone else for the first time since Frieda had known her. While I don't believe that dogs can think in human terms, I have no doubt that they can sense our emotions.

One night, as I was walking on the path with Maria, she started to cry and looked at me with a pleading in her eyes I had not seen before.

"Thank you so much for trying to work it out with Frieda," she said. "I can't bear to think what I would do if you weren't trying so hard to do that."

I told Maria I knew how she felt. I would work it out; I would find a way. I knew Frieda was a great dog with a great heart, and that was how I would approach it.

Frieda was fighting for her life. Maria was her world, and I might well be taking that world away from her. That's an awful lot of emotion for a troubled dog to sort out.

Our first official date came soon after Maria's separation papers were filed. I have blocked out or forgotten a lot of things in my life, but not that sunny late fall afternoon. I called Maria up on a Sunday afternoon at her Granville apartment and asked her to go to lunch at the Anvil Inn, a family restaurant and bar in Fort Edward. She hemmed and hawed a bit, and then she said sure. She came over and we drove together in my car, across the rolling fields and pastures of Washington County.

We were excited, nervous. Outlaws, broken away from the conventions of our lives, from the things that bound us, from the fears that enveloped us. We were there; we were on a date, the first for me in a generation or so.

When we walked into the inn, the hostess immediately recognized me. She asked me about my dogs, told me about her dogs, and looked curiously at Maria. We had both been to the restaurant in our former lives, and the hostess knew something had changed, though perhaps not exactly what.

We both ordered chicken Caesar salads. Maria had a glass of cabernet; I had a Diet Coke. I raised my glass in a toast—I am big on toasts. Maria looked excited and uncertain. But also, and I saw this so clearly at the time, happier than I had ever seen her look.

"We're free," she said. "Aren't we? Is it okay to do this?"

Yes, I said, it is okay to do this. We talked about the adolescent feeling of love, the excitement we felt, the sense of liberation at being able to be together in public. We talked about our divorces, her art, my photography.

For the first time since I had known her, Maria said, "I can't wait to get to work on my quilts." She looked as if a cement bag had been pulled off her shoulders. She also looked as if the police would come crashing through the door any second and arrest us. Sitting across from me, she looked radiant and wonderful—perhaps, I thought, the most wonderful and beautiful thing I had ever seen in my life.

"I'm a little nervous," she said. "Is this okay? Are we allowed to do this?"

How lucky, I thought. How lucky. If I am struck down tomorrow, at least I had this.

And then the hostess came over to ask if everything was all right. Everything was great, I said.

"Dorothy," I said, "have you met Maria? She's my girlfriend."

And in this modest family restaurant, with the TV blaring the overheated pronouncements of an NFL broadcaster, I told Maria that I wanted to get married and have a child with her. Astonished, Maria burst out laughing. "No," she said. "On the first date?"

"Well," I said, "I would." And I did want to get married; I had wanted to marry her even before she had gotten separated.

It sometimes seemed as if Frieda had declared war on Bedlam Farm and its James Herriot–like denizens, that her mission in life was to drive us away from Maria. I had some strict rules about the animals here. If there was one thing I prided myself on, one thing that had emerged as a constant amid all the change and chaos on the farm in the past few years, it was the gentle spirit that suffused the place. I did not tolerate aggressive creatures. In my experience, animals that are well cared for and decently treated have no reason to fight. So there was the sense of the peaceable kingdom on the farm, and Frieda was an anomaly.

I had never experienced that kind of aggression. It was difficult for me to deal with.

Winston the rooster was one of the first symbols of the farm, and he loved the dogs and often followed us around on our walks. He took the guarding of his hens seriously, but I think he sometimes believed he was a dog. He loved to sleep at night with a barn cat cuddled up nearby, and I used to see him napping in the yard next to Orson, my normally arousable border collie.

Mother the barn cat was a ruthless tormenter and killer of mice, rats, and birds, but she rubbed noses with the dogs and loved herding sheep with us up in the pasture.

The donkeys and the dogs got along, and there was a friendly and affectionate spirit at the farm. I was careful to bring only animals who were gentle and easy here, and then gave them no reason to be otherwise. They had plenty to eat, good shelter, fresh water. I think animals pick up on the tone people set. On Bedlam Farm it was quite common to see a rooster walking up to a donkey who had a barn cat wrapped around her feet, a dog sniffing the grass nearby.

No animal on the farm had ever harmed another animal, except once. One day my rooster Winston's powerful young son, Winston Jr., attacked his father and nearly killed him. I was furious. I got the .22 out and shot him on the spot. He had violated his contract to live here. It's just not something I allow on the farm.

Frieda landed on this community like a bomb. A dog who had been kept from people and animals was now plunged into a busy and public place. One morning, Maria and I took Frieda up the hill with Lenore, the one dog she seemed to tolerate, and as usual, Mother followed us—she always accompanied us on our walks. Frieda turned suddenly and lunged for Mother, seizing the barn cat in her paws. Fortunately, Maria was close by and grabbed Frieda by the collar and pulled her off the cat as Mother, stunned, rushed off down the hill. She has never again walked with us, not to this day.

The good news was that Frieda didn't bite me, and she so easily could have. The bad news was that my whole idea of the farm was in danger. She had gone after Rose, the chickens, the donkeys. I didn't even want to think about what would happen if she went after the sheep.

A whole new element had been injected into the farm.

It was time, I knew, to try to get a grip on things.

Chapter Eight

The Beef Jerky Campaign

When Maria left for work one morning—she would often stop by to drop Frieda off, because she was afraid to leave her barking in her apartment all day—I went to write in my study, which was next to the corral where Frieda would stay during the day, until Maria came home. Frieda would erupt whenever trucks went by, or when something moved out in the valley that she didn't like, but mostly she was quiet. There was a red wooden shed in her pen where she could go if it rained or the sun got too strong, a bucket of water, and a chain-link fence that would have held back a small tiger.

I could write in peace—or so I thought until I sat down at my desk and was hit by the fierce and stinging odor of skunk.

It was close and it was strong, and I gagged. I ran out the

back door, and there was Frieda, inside her compound, play-fully flipping a dead skunk up in the air, catching it, and then flipping it up again, as if it were some sort of fuzzy throw toy.

I had never seen Frieda quite so playful or happy before, and if I hadn't been about to get sick from the stench, I would have laughed. Either the skunk had foolishly wandered into Frieda's little compound or Frieda had found its nest and dug it out. Frieda's eyes were running and she was foaming at the mouth a bit from the smell, but if she was uncomfortable in any way, she wasn't acting like it. I went to brew the tomato-and-lemon-juice concoction I used for skunked dogs.

"Frieda," I said, heading for the pantry, "you are a mayhem machine." Then I remembered that there was no way Frieda would let me take the skunk away and wipe her head with to-mato juice.

I looked at my watch. Maria would be back in three hours. Maybe I'd go into town and do some chores.

As I went back to my desk to turn the computer off, I looked out the window and saw the skunk flying up and down through the air. This was different, I thought. I had never seen a dog play with a dead skunk. It would absolutely horrify Rose, who would deem it unprofessional at best, and any Labs I'd ever had would probably have tried to make friends and play with any skunk that crossed their path, dead or alive.

The Beef Jerky Campaign, as I first envisioned it, was simple. It recognized the true food-centered nature of dogs, as well as some of the most important elements of training: be consistent, be clear, be patient, be positive.

I'd learned through my research that most trainers believe it takes about two thousand repetitions for a dog to truly grasp a new behavior. Few people I know, including me, have that kind of patience. But in my experience, food is the foundation of love for a dog, attention being a close second in terms of importance.

So I went online and ordered $500 worth of beef jerky. Beef jerky is expensive. If I was going to follow through on my two thousand repetitions, I'd be spending a lot more than that. I was convinced it was worth it.

One snowy day, Maria left Frieda in the studio barn. Without announcing my intentions (Maria got nervous when I talked about training Frieda, because she thought I might be rough on her; I thought it might be the other way around), I commenced the campaign.

I opened the studio barn's door and walked over to Frieda's crate on the far side, near the woodstove. She was barking, lunging, and roaring. I stood still until she quieted a bit, which took about fifteen minutes. Then I opened a package of beef jerky and tossed a few strips onto the floor.

Frieda doesn't give it away, and she is no pushover for food, but she is a dog, after all, and I thought beef jerky would definitely get her attention. It did.

I walked slowly to the crate, leaned forward and lifted the latch, then let the door swing open. Frieda showed her teeth and lunged. I slid a chair between me and her and backed up quickly until I was safely out the door. Even outside, I could hear Frieda repeatedly throwing herself against the closed door.

I waited a few minutes, until things were quiet; then I opened the door again, tossed in some beef jerky, and slammed it shut. I walked slowly away. The Beef Jerky Campaign was officially under way.

From the first, I was consistent. Frieda sniffed the beef jerky but did not eat it, coming as it had from a man she was determined to keep away from her mistress. Frieda is the proverbial one-person dog, and she was not impressed with me, not as a human, a trainer, a friend of Maria's, or an author of many dog books.

I saw this not as a test of her but of me. Was I patient enough? Could I overcome my fear of this dog, who was intimidating, even menacing? If I didn't, would Maria drift away, start spending more time in her Granville apartment, leave me one day?

Would I get Frieda even more agitated? Damage her even further? And if my plan didn't work, then what? Would Frieda spend the rest of her life in the barn, outside in the winter, apart from Maria, isolated for the rest of her life?

I read some of my favorite dog authors—Patricia McConnell, James Serpell, Stanley Coren—and boned up on body language, dog attention spans, arousal (the excited mental state in dogs that can lead to aggression), and calming training.

For the first two weeks, I walked up to the studio barn (or the fenced-in area, when she was there) every single day. I said her name softly. I held up some beef jerky. And then I ran.

The power of beef jerky over dogs should never be underestimated. Yes, they love us, but they love beef jerky, too. And, I reasoned, eventually they would love the person who brings it.

I did not think Frieda would bite or harm me. But I didn't want to give her the chance to screw up.

My training philosophy has evolved from a hodgepodge of

experience, common sense, reading and research, and anecdotes from other people. Mostly, I follow my own gut instincts.

I reasoned that if I could stay calm, dispensing beef jerky every day would alter Frieda's experience with me. It would enable her over time to see me as nothing but positive. Food is calming for dogs, so our encounters would be calming. And, most important, I would not give her the chance to develop a bad habit—biting me, for example, or running off. All she had to do, all I was asking her to do, was eat the beef jerky. The first few days, she wouldn't touch it. Sometime during the second week, I noticed that it was gone when I returned.

I told Maria what I was doing and asked her to leave Frieda out of the crate because I wasn't sure I'd always have the speed and agility to make it out of the studio barn after I opened the crate and before Frieda demonstrated her impressive security skills. I had been lucky so far, but I didn't want to risk being mauled. After a few weeks, I began to see progress. Frieda barked, but she didn't lunge at the door. She was beginning to get more focused on the good news—the rain of beef jerky strips—than the bad news: me coming into her space.

I never approached her. I just opened the door, said hi, tossed some beef jerky at her, and stood still. She growled and grumbled but also sniffed the beef jerky. I waited until she was calm, then slowly walked out.

This boring pattern became the routine for several weeks. Once I picked up a lead and moved toward her, but she growled and barked, so I backed off.

In many ways, Frieda reminded me of Rose. She was incorruptible, had a ferocious work ethic, and didn't make deals or compromises. I had to steel myself to accept the notion that training her would take a while. I did not for a second imagine that it would take a year. But I did understand that we'd be at it for a long time, and the test was really of my patience, not her temperament.

Frieda had clearly been trained to guard a boundary, and the door to the studio barn was the boundary for the moment. My strategy got simpler, not more complex.

Be calm. Be patient. Be the bringer of beef jerky.

Ask nothing of Frieda, not yet.

My thinking was that if Frieda saw me with beef jerky hundreds, even thousands of times, she would begin to associate me with sweet-smelling meat, always a good thing to a dog, and an important thing.

Dogs love tradition, and this was the tradition I wanted Frieda to come to know.

I spoke to her softly and repeatedly, chatting about the weather, my work. And then I caught a break from the nasty upstate New York winters. It snowed heavily. This didn't prevent Maria, at five A.M., from driving to work in her tiny little Yaris (she refused to borrow my four-wheel-drive truck because she needed, she said, to know she could do it herself) and dropping Frieda off on the way.

But the snow was soon so deep that it gave me another idea. I knew that Frieda, like all dogs—actually, more than most dogs—wanted to go out all the time, so I dug a path from the studio barn right up to the road and made a clearing there, between the road and the barn. I wouldn't need a leash, since she would have nowhere to go other than the clearing, unless she wanted to dig her way out.

Now I had another option. Frieda was an intensely curious and alert dog—part of her intense protective instinct made her want to see what was going on outside. So I opened the door, displayed the beef jerky, and stepped back. Frieda was confused by this. I had removed the boundary.

I stood outside in the snow and wind for a few minutes and called her name, acting as if I were in charge and knew she would obey. (This was not the case.) The drifts were five or six feet high, so I knew she wouldn't go anywhere.

Eventually she came out, sniffing, growling, and looking around. This was great, I thought: a breakthrough, another good thing to associate me with, another chink in her refusal to accept commands from me.

Suddenly, Frieda stiffened and turned. Far down in the meadow below, I spotted a family of deer moving slowly through the snow. So did she.

"No!" I yelled, as people foolishly do when dogs are about to ignore them; but I was sure Frieda wouldn't get over that drift.

She didn't, actually; she simply went right through it, as easily as one of the town's giant plow trucks. Before I could mumble anything else, she was off and down into the meadow, vanishing, along with the deer, in the swirling snow.

So now, I thought, with a rising sense of panic, Maria would come home from work and find that her beloved dog was lost in the woods in the middle of a storm. Good Lord. That would not be helpful.

I walked as far down as I could get—it wasn't far. I didn't

see or hear anything: no tracks, no barking. It was as if she had simply melted into the storm.

Maria had told me about several other occasions when Frieda had run off, and it was the same story every time: she saw something and then just vanished. She always came back, Maria said, wounded and bleeding or with blood caked all over her from something else.

But this was alarming. The storm was just getting under way, and it was going to be bitterly cold, with another five or six inches of snow still coming.

I went into the house, put heavy boots on, and walked the woods for an hour or so. No tracks, no sound, nothing.

The storm got worse, and I hated to think of any dog wandering around out there. Frieda wasn't familiar with these woods. I imagined Maria and me searching for days, then spending years wondering if Frieda had frozen to death, been attacked by coyotes, gotten caught in brambles or barbed wire. The woods were dense out there, even without snow.

I began to panic. This wasn't good. This wasn't the way to begin a relationship with the woman of my dreams.

I filled a thermos with tea and wandered the woods some more. The wind was howling now. I got hay to the donkeys and let the other dogs out by the side of the house. They rushed outside and then immediately back in. None of my dogs wanted anything to do with this storm. Meanwhile, Frieda had been gone for four hours.

I headed out again to look for her, circled down as far as I could get on the path, and then back behind the studio barn, where she had taken off. The door was open a crack, so I went to close it; I didn't want all of the heat to get out.

I clambered up and put my hand on the door and heard a low growl. When I pushed the door open, I was startled to see Frieda, lying on her side in front of the woodstove, covered in a crust of snow and ice, panting heavily.

"Frieda," I said. "You came back!"

Something about my tone caused her to stop growling, and she turned and looked at me, as if assessing me for the very first time. I forgot to be afraid of her, I was so relieved and overjoyed that she had returned.

But then she started to get to her feet. I heard the town plow truck coming down the hill, and I got to the door just before she did.

Well, the good news, I told myself, is that when Maria comes home, I don't have to tell her that Frieda is missing in the woods during the storm of the century. The bad news was that I was not as clever as I'd thought. I seemed to be back at square one.

The laws of dog training are inconsistent, to say the least. While the books are all pretty clear—do x and expect y as a result—Katz's law states that training absolutes break down under the weight of reality and divergent circumstances.

Every dog is different, every home is different, every trainer and street and neighborhood is different.

Two things were becoming very clear to me.

Frieda was a guard dog.

Frieda was a hunter.

She protected Maria and her immediate surroundings with a fierce focus and will. She was ever vigilant, eyes, ears, body moving with every sound, whether engine, breeze, or animal, stirring out in the fields.

Wherever she was, she drew a boundary in front of her and refused to allow any living thing to cross it. She was one of the most dominant dogs I have ever seen.

Beyond that, it was clear that she didn't hunt for fun. My Labs and border collies love to chase deer and chipmunks, for about fifteen feet. All dogs are predators, but some breeds are far from the wild. Dogs that are fed every day for years lose the will or the drive to pursue a rabbit into the deep woods. It takes a lot of running and digging and prey drive to run a wild animal down.

Frieda had what I could only call a ravenous nature. Whether she ate or not, she was always on the alert for prey. I know dogs are descended from wolves, but I had never had a dog like Frieda, and this part of the canine experience was alien to me.

One sunny day we were walking down the path when Frieda suddenly froze, then veered off the trail, pulling Maria along with her. She had found a rabbit den.

The screaming and growling and tearing did not last long. I'll spare you the details about what Frieda did to the mother and her baby bunnies. Maria is one of the most sensitive human beings I have ever known, and this was an awful thing for her to see.

Living on the farm, I had encountered a fair share of death, but not this kind of death. Frieda came up wild-eyed, her snout smeared with blood, her mouth foaming.

Maria covered her eyes and turned away.

I felt so bad for her. I realized how much Maria must love

Frieda, to keep a dog who could do this, and to see that she was not a monster but simply an animal doing what came naturally, and what I suspected she had done to survive in the past.

I felt bad for the rabbits, too, but the sight also jolted me out of any complacency I might have had. I thought of the sweet Labs I'd had over the years, and my bright, energetic, and almost obsessively obedient border collies.

Realistically, the idea of training a rottweiler-shepherd mix who had roamed wild in the Adirondacks and eagerly sought to drive me off the earth might have seemed unlikely.

But I am Churchillian when it comes to daunting tasks. The pursuit of Maria had begun, and so had the Beef Jerky Campaign.

Frieda was starting to pay attention to me now—well, starting to think about doing so, anyway—and she almost always kept her eye on my pockets. My mission was to get closer, to spend more time with her, to get a leash on her, to take her for walks, to begin basic obedience training. What I needed to do now was the same thing I needed to do with Maria. Patience. Don't push it. Let everybody get used to me.

By the end of the year, I wanted both Maria and Frieda to be living in the farmhouse.

Chapter Nine

The Show-Your-Art Guru

Our first night together.

We were both so nervous, like schoolkids meeting in the tree house for the first time. It seemed so natural, and yet so strange to have this woman in my bed.

Most of the people we had known had vanished from our lives, uncomfortable perhaps at the inexplicable choices we made. I had learned in my hospice volunteer work that many people shy away from trouble, but I was not prepared for that to happen to me. I should have been; we lived in a small town, after all, and in small towns people run from that kind of trouble. We felt very much alone. But also very much alone together.

Frieda had been in the studio barn that day and was still

there in the evening—Maria ran over every few hours to check on the woodstove, make sure it was warm enough in there, ferrying biscuits back and forth.

She would look out the window across the snowy road and ask, "Do you think she's all right over there?" Sure, I'd say, she's a dog. But nobody likes to see their dog sleeping in a barn on a cold night in a storm, even if there's a woodstove there.

I had the feeling that Maria might spend the night if I suggested it gently and quietly. It was snowing heavily, and she was exhausted—she'd gone to her job at five A.M. and had worked all day on her quilts. She'd had a few glasses of wine, and Frieda was tucked in safely across the street. At first, she said no, but then I saw her nodding off, and she came over to the couch and curled up with me and we just held each other in the warmest and most loving way. Both of us were crying, not in sorrow but in inexpressible joy at being together on this wintry night in front of a hot woodstove. Izzy, Rose, and Lenore were tucked away in various corners of the house, warm and comfortable. We both felt bad for Frieda. "She'll never be able to come in the house, will she?" Maria asked. And I told her the truth—I said I didn't know.

Maria was very wary of staying at the farm. She didn't want people to know about us—it's a small town, so of course everyone would find out—because they might think we had been plotting an affair all along. She didn't want to be seen as running to me, hiding in the farmhouse.

So after that first night, she hid her car in the barn when

she stayed over. Or behind the farmhouse, in an elaborate ruse that made me smile. The day before, I had gone to the town general store to buy some milk, and the woman working there, whom I had never seen before, smiled when I came in. "Got some visitors up on the farm, eh?"

Maria would have jumped out of her shoes if I had told her that.

She didn't want to become dependent on me, or lose her identity. She prized her little Granville apartment, even though she could barely turn around in there and Frieda could not be left alone, for fear of the din she would raise.

Maria had almost no money, but she would not take a cent from me, and we could go out to eat only if she could pay every other time, or half each time, and this sent us to some faraway dumps that specialized in pasta and soup.

I could see how tired she was that first night. She had gotten up at five that morning and would be getting up at five the next. Maria was still working at the home for emotionally disabled people, whose frustrations often took the form of throwing things at her or giving her a punch or a kick.

She was exhausted, as well as broke, frightened, and bewildered by the choices she now had to make, different ones than she had imagined even a few months ago.

She wanted to pay her own way, yet the rent in Granville was eating up her meager earnings, barely above minimum wage. She couldn't give Frieda up, yet there was no way she could live with her in the apartment. And she couldn't afford to buy the sewing machine she needed to produce her art.

If she moved to the farm, at least she could save the rent

money, half of what she was earning. I didn't think our being together was really the issue, because we always loved being together.

She desperately wanted to resume her art, and she had the great temptation of the studio barn, yet she was not about to become Mrs. Bedlam Farm. Through the prism of her life, I began to see my own more clearly. To think about what I needed, rather than what I bought. To wait for things I wanted. To see the lives of other people more empathetically. To open up and look at my life.

Maria was not living at my farm, but she was transforming it. Beautiful rocks and feathers appeared on windowsills in the farmhouse. Flowers sprouted on my desk, in the bathroom, by the doors. I had bought furniture but did not see how cold and empty the farmhouse was until Maria brought her presence and creativity to it. I saw it come to life, sprout color, reflect the earth and the world around it. Just as she was doing for me, just as was happening to me.

I was coming to life.

More than anything, I wanted to be with Maria all the time, to live with her at the farm, to share my life, to support her work. More than at any time in my life, I needed to shut up, be quiet, let her come to her own mind. Just like I needed to do with Frieda. If I was to have them in my life, I would have to change. To wait. To listen to them. To accept them. To redefine my whole notion of patience and delayed expectations. And, sure, of loneliness.

I had often heard women complain that most men just wanted someone to take care of them. A neighbor, a friend in her sixties, told me after her husband died that she would never marry again. She was done taking care of men. I didn't want Maria to take care of me. I wanted us to take care of each other.

And there was something else, something that Maria didn't understand and doesn't yet understand, because it's just not the way she thinks. Because those seventeen years between us are big ones, even if they are not important to her.

But if you are over sixty, and your feet hurt, and walking up hills requires some concentration and planning, and you run to the bathroom a lot, you have a different sense of time.

I am not often gloomy about aging—quite the opposite. I am much better at being older than being younger. But I also know that I do not have decades to ponder my need for love or companionship, or my ferocious wish to live my life more fully. That's the trouble with awakenings; you are awake to the urgency of living well.

And that's the trouble with love. If you have not had it, and you sniff it, then you are just like a dog, just like Frieda: you are on the hunt, and nobody can tell you to calm down and take the long view. Because the long view is not that long for me. I was not a teenager or a newlywed with a half century ahead of me in which to sort things out. I don't see this as depressing, just realistic. A call to make use of my time and not be defined by the suffocating expectations of other people.

I have made a lot of noise about the dangers of comparing dogs to humans, and I don't believe in it. They are not like us, but sometimes they do challenge us in the same ways, teach us new things.

Being patient with Maria was, in fact, like training a dog. If I wanted to be with these two idiosyncratic, sometimes difficult females—and I did—I had to be a better human. To really learn patience. To understand that love is about not just what I want, but what someone else wants. This is something I wished I had learned earlier in life, but it's never too late, and I wanted to embrace it now.

More than anything, Maria hoped to revive her life as an artist, to make her quilts, to work in her studio barn. Moving into the farmhouse was her best shot at that, yet she understood that it shouldn't be the only reason.

She had to be sure about us. I appreciated the tough spot she was in. I just wanted to be with her, and if I had to move to Granville, so be it. She laughed at that suggestion. Where would I put the dogs? What about the donkeys?

But if she came to the farm, lived with me, and never knew that she could be independent, figure out life, take care of herself, then that would not be good for us, either, together or apart. And I had to be careful not to do anything to undermine her still-fragile sense of confidence.

I sat there on that first night, listening to the fire crackle in the woodstove, happy to be in the big old living room of my farmhouse, with Izzy, Lenore, and Rose draped off in corners dozing, talking to Maria about our lives, watching her droop in exhaustion. She kept asking me if I thought Frieda was okay. But I had only two thoughts (which I kept to myself): (1) Somehow, I had to get Frieda to live in the farmhouse; (2) Please, God, let Maria stay over.

I walked with her across the road to check on Frieda. She came running out of her crate for Maria, and pressed her head into Maria's hand. She tossed me a rumbly growl, but she was too excited at the prospect of taking a walk with Maria to bother with me much.

"Get busy," Maria said, and Frieda did; then we put her back into the studio barn to spend the night out in the storm by herself.

"She's warm," I said. "She's okay." Maria nodded, looking back.

I don't think Maria could have made it to Granville that night even if she'd wanted to. She could hardly keep her eyes open, snow and ice were building up on the roads, and she had to get up in a few hours to go to work.

Just shut up, I told myself, and she'll stay here. Don't ask her to decide. So I didn't. She didn't really decide to stay; she more or less collapsed into sleep.

I was terrified but ready. I'd brought some flowers up into my bedroom. I'd put a CD in my boom box, a mix of brooding old songs—Van Morrison, Tom Waits, Sarah McLachlan— that I loved. It had been a long time since anyone but me and Lenore had slept in that bed. I got Lenore when she was eight weeks old, and within a month she was curled up in a little ball at the foot of the bed, where she spent the night, snoring some- times but hardly moving.

When I was lonely or frightened, which was often, I would reach out and put my hand on her back and she would turn around and lick my fingers, and I would sing a song to her— usually "You Light Up My Life"—and she brightened many a dark and achingly lonely night. I explained to Lenore that we might have company that evening.

So Maria stayed at the farmhouse that night, and my life changed. I'd thought this kind of thing was far behind me, and

I had no idea what to say or to do. I told myself to be natural, be honest, be me. I helped Lenore climb up into her usual spot; she looked at Maria, who was undressed and in bed before me, wagged her tail, and went to sleep. Labs are flexible as long as they are well-fed and comfortable.

Before I got into bed, I put the CD on, Tom Waits singing a heart-wrenching and lonely version of "Waltzing Matilda."

I got into bed as the CD played, and all the sorrow and sadness and loss of my life seemed to rush out of me into a cloud, and up into the dark night. I burst into tears.

"Oh," Maria said, taking me in her arms. "So sad."

"No, no," I said. Not anymore.

Maria stayed on the farm more often after that. Each night she would announce that she and Frieda were heading back into Granville, back to the apartment. But I would cook some pasta or fish, and we would take a walk, and we'd talk and talk, and she would have some wine, which I was careful to keep stocked in a cabinet in the kitchen, and then we would walk Frieda again around ten P.M., when Maria began to get groggy.

Maria had so little; I understood why she was wary of Bedlam Farm and all the stuff in it. She had never had a cellphone, a computer, or clothes that didn't come from a thrift shop, and I was worried about her driving along the country roads by herself in her little toilet bowl Yaris (which didn't have snow tires or four-wheel drive), so I pestered and whined until she at least agreed to get a phone. We drove to Saratoga Springs to purchase her first cell. The salesman paled when he realized she didn't know what "minutes" meant, and before she could glower at me, I went to wait for her outside. She was fascinated by the phone, looked at it as if it had fallen out of a spaceship, was startled to discover that she could call her mother on it from anywhere, that she didn't have to be at home calling from a landline.

She brought it with her when she took Frieda out by herself, and on our walks with the dogs, in case anything might happen.

I sensed a change in Frieda after we'd taken a few of these walks. I was something different. I think she was figuring out that I was not so much an intruder as a resident, perhaps even something to worry about or protect. Frieda at her core is a generous soul, and if she loves you, she watches out for you. If she doesn't, then you belong in that dark world of intruders to be driven away.

Frieda and I were not quite friends yet, but the barking and growling had grown less intense, less intimidating. It seemed more a matter of form, of pride. If I reached over to Frieda to put a leash on her, she would growl, even snap at me. So I didn't. But on the walks, I noticed for the first time, she was more interested in sniffing for scents and animals than she was in eating me.

When Maria stayed over, we settled into a new and wonderful routine. I would get up at four-thirty and make breakfast while she showered and dressed. I had done little cooking in my previous life, but I found that I loved shopping and cooking for Maria. I discovered that she loved oatmeal and toast. I drove to the Saratoga supermarket and got grapefruits and oranges. I experimented with goat cheese and hummus, oat bran and bagels, fried eggs and fruit.

When she came down, I would have coffee and tea ready and we would sit in the living room and talk about the day, share our plans. More than anything, Maria spoke about coming home from work and making her art. She was changing, coming to life.

"I feel like I've been shut down all of my life," she said. "I've always wanted to be an artist—I studied art in school, worked in a museum. I just got lost." She said the studio barn meant the world to her.

And then, sometimes, she would just burst into tears, and smile.

"I cry a lot," she said.

"I know," I said.

"Does it bother you?" she asked.

"No, it doesn't. It means you are alive, you have feelings. In fact," I said, "every time you cry, I love you a bit more."

She cried at that.

"How do I know you are for real?" she asked. "How do I know you mean it?"

"You don't," I said. "You will just have to wait and see. My job is to convince you."

In the studio barn, she was making quilts out of discarded fabric. I loved to go and sit and watch her work—it seemed to me that here, I was seeing the real Maria emerge. She laughed, whistled, danced, and sang, rushing from one box of fabric to another, and then to the sewing machine she had gotten from her mother. It was magical, like watching a human being grow into herself right in front of you.

The problem was that she had given up on the idea of showing her art to people. That prospect frightened her, and while she loved making things, she couldn't imagine showing them, selling them, offering them to the world.

This was not a small matter, for her or for us. Maria had begun to think that she ought to get a full-time job, pay her way in the world, prove that she could take care of herself. The art wasn't going to work, she thought. Nobody would like it. Nobody would buy it. The economy was crashing around us, and the air was filled with bad news about people and money, and many of the artists and writers we both knew were heading for higher ground, taking part-time jobs, teaching, or giving up.

Maria had what the shrinks love to call low self-esteem, which was a generous way of putting it. The idea of taking a chance and doing her art and selling it seemed an almost impossible—and terrifying—stretch for her.

She had to give it a shot, I argued. She had to give making a living as an artist a chance. She could start a blog, we would go to shows together, she could visit shops and galleries in Vermont and Saratoga and Glens Falls. She seesawed back and forth each day. I could not imagine Maria giving up her art again.

I had a plan.

One winter morning, when Maria came down for breakfast, I was wearing a huge blue terry-cloth bathrobe and a big blue wizard hat, which actually had a battery that caused red and blue LED lights embedded in the hat to twinkle. A home-made wand fashioned out of a twig I had pulled off a tree completed the effect.

"God," said Maria, laughing, breaking into her wide and beautiful smile. "What are you?"

I bowed and rose with gravity. "I am the Show-Your-Art Guru," I said, with great seriousness. "I am here with my magic hat and wand to help you show your art."

I can't quite imagine the sight I must have been, rushing around in my bathrobe and wizard's hat, chanting and singing. Maria cracked up, shaking her head.

"What are we going to do with you?" she asked.

"How about marrying me?" I suggested helpfully. "Moving in?"

Maria looked at me, a bit shocked, puzzled, uneasy. Then she laughed. She didn't say yes. She didn't say no. She just laughed. As if I had suggested flying to the moon after lunch.

Maria is nothing if not polite and courteous to a fault, so I wasn't hurt by her laughter. My guess was that she just had no idea what to say.

So I dropped it.

Life is strange and life is wonderful. The appearance of the Show-Your-Art Guru seemed to touch Maria, embolden her in some way.

Most mornings when she came down, she had to confront this bizarre apparition, a large man in a bathrobe and wizard hat in a kitchen in the middle of nowhere in the middle of winter, chanting and singing songs about her art.

A few weeks later, she took some of her quilts to a gallery in

Dorset, Vermont. The owner loved them and agreed to put several of them up. Somebody bought one soon after.

And what of our Frieda?

Frieda was the crazed guardian of the studio barn. She spent her days and nights there, either in her crate or outside it when Maria was around. If she saw my dogs, she would literally foam at the mouth, charging toward them, barking and roaring, losing her mind. She was not allowed near them or the farm animals, who elicited more or less the same response. So did kids in the street, loud trucks, motorcycles, people walking dogs, airplanes, and sirens.

I had never known a dog as vigilant as Frieda or one with her almost supernatural instincts. She could sense or hear a dog approaching from a half mile away, or a kid setting out for the school bus a quarter of a mile up the road.

She not only locked onto my dogs, she fixated on the dogs who were walked up the road every day, especially Teddy, a small poodle whose owner took him out each morning at six, and Dakota, a husky whose owner walked him morning and night by the farmhouse. She watched for them all day long. She began barking and lunging long before the dogs appeared. When they came near, she would explode in a fit of barking and growling, lunging at the crate.

I know that barking dogs are especially happy when dogs or letter carriers go by, because each time they leave, the dog feels affirmed and successful. Driving dangers away is one of the many gifts dogs give us, and Frieda was definitely vice president of security. If she were online, she would be dispensing passwords and PINs and building firewalls all day. And nobody would get through, either.

In the country, things are informal. Sometimes Kirk, the UPS driver, would ask if he could use the bathroom in the farmhouse. After a few months, I told him to just come in; he didn't need to ask.

Kirk loved my dogs and always had treats for them. He would pause at the gate for them to sniff and lick him. Once Lenore came out and jumped into his truck, and the two of them rode around for a while before he brought her back. Lenore loves Kirk.

One morning when I was away, Maria was walking Frieda around the back driveway so that she wouldn't lunge at my dogs, who were milling around the front yard.

I hadn't told Kirk about Frieda—he had only just figured out that Maria and I were an item after he'd started delivering art supplies to the house—and he'd stopped in to use the bathroom. As Kirk told the story, he heard this roar, looked up, and saw a "monster dog" hurtling at him at full speed. He threw an Amazon box on the ground to slow her down—it didn't—and he only just made it back to the truck and slammed the door before Frieda got there, clawing at the door, trying to get at his leg, with Maria rushing up right behind her.

Kirk laughed about it later, describing the incident to me. It was his fault, he said; he should have called out and announced his presence.

"She isn't like Lenore, is she?" he asked.

No, I agreed, not like Lenore.

Chapter Ten

Willfulness and Progress

One winter afternoon, Maria left the studio barn and was walking across the road to the farmhouse when a stray dog came charging up the hill, barking. Frieda rushed out of her open crate and slipped through the wobbly wooden frame door at the side of the barn. She ran straight to Maria and positioned herself between the stray and her human. The dog took one look at Frieda, froze, and then turned and ran. Maria got her hands on Frieda before she took off after the stray.

When Maria went back to examine it, the bottom of the door was splintered. Frieda had just put her head down and exploded right through the wooden frame. And that was the thing about Frieda, the thing I kept remembering when I wanted to strangle her. Her devotion was touching, even inspiring. There was no doubt in my mind that Frieda would lay down her life for Maria in an instant, without hesitation. And I kept remembering that this devotion was a beautiful thing. I just had to figure out how to make it work for Frieda and me.

The winter of 2009 was grim, even by the tough standards of upstate New York. It snowed from November to March, the worst storms always seeming to fall on Sundays. Maria began spending more time at the farm. We didn't comment on it or analyze what it meant; I just kept my mouth shut and it began to happen. She loved being in the studio barn, hated her Granville apartment, and was thrilled to be making her art. We loved being together, talking, laughing, sharing our work and the farm chores.

On Sundays, Maria worked a brutal twelve-hour shift at the group home that often involved driving the residents long distances to see relatives, shop, or go to amusement parks.

I hated these days, for several reasons. I missed Maria, but also, although I didn't say so, it felt like I was alone on the farm again, for another winter. There is no sugarcoating it: winters alone upstate are unrelenting and bleak. These Sundays brought me back to a place I didn't ever wish to return to.

Also, I hated to see Maria head off in a storm in a car that had no snow tires or four-wheel drive. It was as light as a lawn mower. Every winter we hear reports of awful skids and crashes, usually involving the small sedans relied on by working people who can't afford four-wheel drive. The cars have no traction or weight to stabilize them on black ice or in other hazardous conditions. Maria wouldn't stand much chance against a pickup if her Yaris slid off the road or across a lane. Those Sunday blizzards were awful, the car was tiny, and I had twelve hours to worry about it all.

Maria was very, very independent. She did not call me to tell me she had arrived, was okay, or was en route. I'd find out she was all right when she got home, sometime around eight P.M.

Every Sunday, we woke up to heavy snows and drifts. Every Sunday, I begged her to take my truck. Or get snow tires. Or borrow somebody else's car. Every Sunday, she refused. She wanted to make it on her own. She wanted to know she could do it.

I argued and pleaded. Why did she need to know she could slide into a ditch and be stuck there for hours? Or run into a pole or an embankment? Or another car or truck? Why not skip that particular experience of enlightenment? I got nowhere.

It was her life. I didn't get to have a say.

I had twelve hours to fill, and I wasn't going anywhere. The snow had really accumulated. The roads would not be plowed for hours, and I couldn't get out, not even in my four-wheel-drive truck.

And then there was Frieda. She had to be let out, walked and exercised, even in the snow.

I told Maria to tie a long rope on her and leave her out of the crate. Normally, Frieda was walked on a leash, but a rope was longer, and if it was tied to her, I could just pick up the end and walk her without having to reach for her throat—a bad idea at that point. In this way, she could get used to walking with me and I could keep her from tearing off into the woods or after cars, trucks, or people. Thanks to the Beef Jerky Campaign, she had calmed down around me a bit. And she loved walks.

She was no longer charging the door when I showed up, just quietly glowering and growling at me. She might even have been a bit glad to see me. She was cooped up in the studio barn for hours, and the beef jerky probably looked (and smelled) pretty good to her.

Soon after Maria drove off, vanishing into the drifts and swirling mists and darkness, I walked Rose, Izzy, and Lenore. After I got the dogs back in the house and rested a bit in front of the woodstove, I put on my boots and parka again and headed over to the studio barn.

I felt for Frieda. The wind was howling through the meadow, the studio barn windows covered in drifting snow. The woodstove was kept burning—my task throughout the day—and the lights were left on, so Frieda wouldn't feel lonely.

The first Sunday Maria stayed with me and left Frieda, I approached the door and heard a low growl, but no bark. Much quieter than usual. Frieda was sitting in her crate, with the door open. I threw some beef jerky on the floor and she got up, sniffed it, and looked at me. I admired Frieda's incorruptibility. Any Lab I have known would have been in my lap after all that beef jerky. Frieda wouldn't even eat it in front of me.

I opened the door, and Frieda walked slowly over to me, looking at the door, the snow, then back at the crate. Then she walked slowly past me, fur up, ears back, but when I leaned over to pick up the rope, she didn't even blink.

A big step. She wouldn't let me approach her, much less touch her. Nor would she obey me or listen to my commands.

But now I could take her outside, and I did. We walked out in the snow for an hour, and although the drifts were deep, I could see that she loved being outside, poking her nose in the snow, looking for rabbit or other animal holes, marking snow mounds, scanning the woods.

We went far down the path, then walked back. We were both covered in snow and ice, which clung to her coat and covered her head. Back into the studio barn, she turned once and looked at me, then walked past the beef jerky and into her crate, where she lay down, to wait for Maria.

I came back three or four times that Sunday, and each time, the beef jerky from the previous visit was gone. Frieda quickly stepped out of her crate, let me bend over near her to pick up the rope, and we went out for a walk. I could see that she looked forward to this, even enjoyed it.

On my third visit, I got cocky. I brought a leash and leaned over to try to clip it to Frieda's collar. She growled, then snapped in the direction of my hand. I had moved too soon. I backed up, grabbed the rope, and we went on our walk.

I was very careful then not to correct Frieda, challenge her, or ask much of her. I wanted her to associate me with good things only—chatter, food, walks.

But on one of the visits, we had a talk.

She met my eyes when I started talking to her, and her ears went up. She was taking me in, absorbing my tone of voice.

Dogs read emotions much better than people do, and I didn't need to tell her what I was thinking or feeling. She sensed my intentions. She knew by then that I was not a danger. But she did not yet know what I was.

"Frieda," I said, "we need to work this out, for both of our sakes. I love Maria, and I want her to live here. And while I don't love you yet, I think I could. You are a brave and loyal creature, and I sense you have quite a backstory and have lived through a lot. I admire the way you watch over Maria. I want to do the same. Maybe one day you will watch out for the farm. In the meantime, I hope we can work together."

Frieda looked me in the eye, tilting her ears at the mention of her name. Dogs have adapted and survived for thousands of years by reading the emotions and moods of humans. That's why they get into our beds and raccoons don't. Animals that make contact with humans—eye contact and physical contact—do well in evolutionary terms. Animals that do not struggle to co-exist with people.

Dogs, cats, donkeys, and horses have lived in close quarters with humans and sense what humans want from them. By instinctively providing it, they have earned a special place in the world. We humans, the most fearsome and destructive of species, project all sorts of things onto them. Dogs are masters of using this to their own advantage. They show some emotions—fear, affection, curiosity—and essentially trick us into thinking they are just like us, and we attach to them, projecting all kinds of ideas into their minds.

Frieda understood Maria well. She would come up to her, look her in the eye, press her head against Maria's knee. Her look was one of great love and gratitude. This invariably touched Maria, deeply. She would respond by talking to Frieda, calling her by name, using a special, high-pitched voice when speaking to her, giving her a treat.

This is the great ballet of the human-canine relationship, and dogs often understand it much better than we do, because they are using their instincts, and we have only our poor and limited intellects.

When Maria thought of Frieda as being cute, it was because Frieda was "cute" with her. Frieda had sensed what Maria needed and wanted her to be—a protector and an affectionate companion—and this was her work, to be both.

Frieda was a working dog, and she had two very protective breeds mixed into her: rottweiler and shepherd. Both have tough reputations; both are known for love and loyalty to single humans or families. When these breeds attach, it is very powerful and usually to a single person.

The Lab has been bred for some of the same qualities, but Labs are also bred for congeniality and flexibility. They like most people, and they love food and the sensual things of their world: mud, dirt, carcasses. Their original breeders wanted dogs who could hang out for hours with fishermen and also participate in the hunt, retrieving game without harming it. Hunting was a social activity, and temperament, congeniality, and responsiveness were important.

Shepherds and rottweilers are naturally loving, but they were not bred to be congenial to everyone, although many are. They are territorial, fiercely loyal, working herders and hunters. Both breeds are valued for security work, as they are very loyal to handlers and can be trained to aggressively pursue enemies or invaders.

I always say that people get the dogs they need, and dogs react to what people need from them. I called Frieda "the Dog Who Kept Men Away" because she was Maria's shield, a reason for Maria to stay out of the world, to avoid meeting and socializing with people.

Dogs sense what is expected of them—their survival depends on it—and Frieda had come to understand her role well. She and Maria had lived isolated lives, and now that world was changing. Another human had entered it, along with dogs and farm animals and traffic and new people.

Frieda was clearly confused. And she was also untrained, in the way dogs who are rescued are sometimes untrained—their owners, good-hearted people like Maria, just can't bear to inflict any more discipline or harm on them. This is understandable, of course. But it is hard on the dogs sometimes, and it is not ultimately loving. Dogs like Frieda—dogs who look dangerous and can sometimes be dangerous—need training desperately. They need to know how to be safe in an often hostile world. And they need to be controlled, their fierce instincts curbed.

Frieda's job had been to keep people away from Maria. Now her job was changing, and the challenge was to communicate this to her, so her intelligence and loyalty and work ethic could be reshaped, redirected, transformed. Not an easy assignment. Maria had no idea how to do it, even though Frieda was sensing the change, and it clearly had frightened and confused her. I believed that dogs are adaptable, that they can be trained or retrained at any age. Now I would get the chance to prove that theory.

I had three dogs I'd needed, and then got. This cannot be coincidence. Dogs read us and can, if they understand us, become what we need them to become, within reason. Most of my dogs—Rose was an exception—have loved to pose for photos, go to readings, greet visitors. Yes, dogs know on which side their bread is buttered. But training is what helps them see it.

Rose the Working Dog. Izzy the Hospice Therapy Dog. Lenore the Love Dog. Each of these dogs had assumed the role I needed them to assume, and had had that reinforced in them. Could I do this with Frieda?

I didn't really know. I had never worked with the powerful rottweiler and shepherd breeds before, either separately or in one big handful of dog. But it was important for me to believe that I could, and for Frieda to see that I believed that. I needed to project confidence, clarity, consistency.

This, then, has become my philosophy of dogs. I am not as certain as Cesar Millan, or as specific as the Monks of New Skete. I cannot read dog behavior the way Patricia McConnell can. But I have some remarkable dogs, and my own philosophy is a curious mishmash of perspective, spirituality, personal experience, patience, clarity, firmness, and love. I am a positive-reinforcement trainer, but I yell at my dogs frequently, especially if they knock me over or run into the road or try to harm one another. Because I am also a human, and we are not perfect.

Training depends on who you are, where you live, how you behave. You can't train a dog if you are pretending to be someone else. They just get confused. If you have three kids and live in a suburb, you cannot train a dog the way I do. Or monks do. Or TV personalities and their large staffs do.

So we all have to make our own blend, our own recipe, be true to ourselves and sensitive to our dogs. It is not a simple thing. You don't do it in five lessons at the Y with a good-citizen certificate. Reading books, watching DVDs, and signing up for lessons are all good things to do, but they are just a beginning, the start of a long process that does not end until you or the dog have gone to glory.

I don't believe, despite all the gurus in the pet section of the bookstore and on TV, that there is a single way to train every dog, any more than that there is one way to buy a dog or put one down. I think this idea causes much grief for dog lovers, as it does for dog choosers.

My idea of what to do with Frieda was becoming clearer as I got to know her. First, show her that I am okay. Second, reinforce that with lots of good food. Third, ask little or nothing of her until she knows and trusts me. However long that takes.

Finally, and most important, Frieda had to understand that she was not in charge of the farm, nor was she responsible for monitoring the comings and goings. The farm was not a hunting ground; nor was it a territory she had to defend. Since no one had asserted authority over Frieda, she thought she was in charge of everything, and because she was a big and strong working dog with a powerful prey drive, most things human and animal were afraid of her.

So it was important that I not be afraid of her, the way my dog Rose was not afraid of her. I had to project confidence and calmness, patience and clarity. I had to build repetition and tradition into her life and our relationship.

I had to show her that I was in charge, not her, so that she could relax and be the loving and loyal dog she was, and not hurt the other dogs or animals (or me or any other human) and be a companion and a pet, not a warrior guardian dog.

"You are carrying too much weight," I told her. "We need to lighten you up."

My other task involved her relationship with Maria. I had to show Frieda—not command her, but show her—that I was not a danger to Maria, not intruding on her life or safety. I wanted Frieda to see me as something added, not something that was taking things away. That is a difficult thing to do with a dog.

I had a couple of tools. Frieda loved Maria and was extraordinarily sensitive to her approval and displeasure. Lenore had charmed her and calmed her, so I would, where possible, bring Lenore into the training.

I was also doing my homework, talking to some trainers I knew, reading some good advice—mostly in academic journals—about dog behavior and instincts.

I had to expose Frieda to the other dogs safely, and I had some ideas about how to do that. I had to do all of this slowly and carefully. I had to believe that I could do it and would do it, so that when Frieda looked into my eyes, or smelled my emotions, she would sense the following things:

- My love for Maria.

- My strength and determination. She had to see that I was stronger than her, smarter than her, and in charge of her.

- My goals and intention. Dogs do not understand words, but they do read intentions. Their existence depends on it. Mine had to be crystal clear in my head for her to get it.

Whenever I approached Frieda, I looked her in the eye and declared my intention: We are going to do this, girl. We are going to work it out. The time it takes may be short or long, the process may be simple or complex, but it is going to happen.

On our first date together, I had asked Maria to marry me. And again after she first slept over, when we were making breakfast in the kitchen. And she laughed. I asked her to marry me every day after that for more than a year. "I can't marry you," she said directly one day. "It's too soon. I'm not ready to get married. Neither are you." I said I respected her decision but disagreed.

Sometimes I called her and left marriage proposals on the voice mail of her new cellphone. Sometimes I brought food into the studio barn and proposed to her there. Sometimes during dinner. Sometimes in the car, driving around.

I left her proposal notes. I was very straightforward, not flowery or long-winded. I just kept asking her to marry me. She just laughed and told me I was crazy.

I suppose I understood on some level that Maria hates to turn anybody down for anything, so it was just possible that I could persuade her over time. More than anything, I wanted her to know how much I loved her.

It was also revealing. Maria seemed to understand that I was odd, but apparently it didn't bother her. Things that annoyed or troubled other people didn't annoy or trouble her. Yet she had a powerful will of her own. If she didn't want to do something, she just didn't do it, and didn't think a thing about it. I was free to be me, understanding that she was not in any way intimidated by me, or even found it necessary to always take me seriously.

Over time, she began to say, "No, thank you, not now." But she still could barely keep from laughing.

This went on for months, and she knew I would ask her and I knew she would say no. But her language changed. It became less definitive, more promising. "Maybe one day," she said, at last.

I was beginning to know Maria, and to understand how much more complex she was than I'd realized when I had first met her. For one thing, she was anything but mute. She had plenty to say. And she was anything but meek. She told me no, all the time, and with little hesitation. My friend Mary Kellogg was right when she said Maria would keep me in line. If I wanted to buy something stupid or do something stupid, Maria was right there in my face. If I was impulsive, she told me to calm down and slow down. If I lost my temper, she told me to wait. I've learned that if you want to survive and prosper in the world, you need to find strong women and do what they tell you. Maria was such a woman.

One afternoon, I looked at my bank account, saw that I was running out of money, and had a massive panic attack. Sweating, dizziness, stomach trouble, running to the bathroom, terror just coursing through my body. Maria sat beside me for hours, holding my hand, helping me breathe, bringing me tea. This was the me I didn't want Frieda to see.

I had panic attacks all the time in those days, and so did Maria. We never got annoyed with each other, never brushed the other's concerns off, never were too busy to deal with a problem, never failed to come up with ways to handle one. And all of those ways were loving, gentle, and helpful.

For most of my life, when I was frightened, I never believed the people who told me it would be all right. But I always believed Maria; she always brought me back, and I always did the same for her. We were on a shared journey of encouragement, support, connection.

Why wouldn't I want to marry her?

But I also well understood why she wasn't ready. If we got married and she didn't know she could care for herself, that would be an unhealthy relationship. She would become afraid and then angry.

A former friend of hers came up to me in a market one day and said, with something of a smirk, "So how's Maria? We don't see much of her lately. Is she up at the farm helping you write?" I have my own issues with anger, but I am definitely not a fighter. Still, I came close to mashing some peaches into his face.

"Actually," I said, "I don't need any help writing. Maria is starting her own fiber arts business." But this was precisely why Maria was so nervous about marrying me. This was what people would say.

Few of the people who were in my life then are in my life now. And I had few people to talk to about Maria and me. Mary Kellogg was one of the few, a witness to our life—an angel, a godmother, a friend. She was the first person I called when I realized I was in love with Maria. "Good choice," said Mary. "She's a wonderful girl. You need each other. Take it slow. You'll get her moving. She will keep you in line."

Not everyone was so supportive.

One woman read Maria's blog and emailed her a long rant about how lucky she was to have this perfect life, to be hanging out with me, to be able to do her art, and not to have to worry about sending kids to college or paying a mortgage by herself. And we weren't even married! the email scolded.

Maria was not yet experienced in the ways of Internet communications, email, and social media. All sorts of unwanted advice, observations, criticism, and inappropriate messages pour in all the time. Maria and I had some long talks about this particular message. This was a person, I said, who did not want to take responsibility for her own life and was looking for something outside of herself to blame for her decisions. Nobody had made her have kids or send them to college. And if you are going to be an artist or a writer, somebody has to buy your work. It's as simple as that.

It's easy to look at someone else's life and label it simple or perfect—email and public comments make it very easy. Ignore it, I said. But Maria couldn't quite ignore it. It touched a nerve. She wrote back. She said her life was not easy, and that the woman who'd written her knew nothing about how perfect it was or wasn't, and then she wrote about it on her blog. All sorts of people posted comments in support of Maria, and then the woman wrote back. Maria learned a lot about the Internet that day—there is much hostility, and there is great support.

You just have to stop answering messages like that, I said. Your life and choices are not arguments for other people to participate in. They are your own. In a way, this foreshadowed and highlighted our life together. Because of my work, our blogs, my books, much of our lives were out in the open. It is a new reality even for public people, and while I was used to it, it was a special challenge for someone as private and shy as she had been.

———

This was a big issue for Maria, and I wanted to treat it respectfully. I also felt strongly that we belonged together. I believe in marriage; I believe in commitment. If something happened to me, I wanted Maria to have the farm, to have some resources so she could do what she wished with her life. This was love to me, and I felt it strongly.

So it was in the air—I kept it there—but without rancor. I didn't argue with her, try to talk her into it, or get annoyed. I just kept asking.

I am not a subtle person. I am not good at waiting. I had lived alone long enough, been loveless long enough, been frightened long enough.

I was done with that.

Chapter Eleven

Brownie

I decided that I needed to learn more about Frieda if I was ever to understand her and successfully train her. The Internet and my blog gave me some new tools, and they worked almost instantly.

After Maria and I began dating, I started writing about Frieda and posting photos of her on my website, bedlamfarm .com. I said I was looking to find anyone who recognized her, knew her, or had seen her before she came to live with Maria. I was seeking information that might help me understand and train her. Very few people who wind up with dogs like Frieda ever get to know the truth about their lives.

They might have some clues about how the dog was treated or learn something from the shelter about the dog's former life.

Usually, that is not the case. Because my blog is widely read locally as well as nationally, I had a reasonably good chance that someone might spot Frieda and recognize her. Gossip and story trading is a religion where I live, so I put Frieda's photo up a few times, wrote about trying to train her, and asked if anyone recognized her.

I knew workers at the shelter where Frieda was kept until Maria adopted her. They agreed to tell me what they could about her. But they didn't know where she had been before she was captured while roaming the grounds at Adirondack Community College.

At this point, Maria was spending a lot of time at the farm. She hadn't officially decided to move in, but we were heading in that direction. I understood by now that the best approach with Maria was not to push her too hard or formalize things. If she wanted to do it, she would come to it herself.

Frieda spent all her days and many nights in the studio. She was becoming a part of the household, even if she still seemed at war with it. I was still proposing to Maria, and she was still politely telling me no thanks, not yet.

A few weeks after I put the first pictures of Frieda up, Stella, from nearby South Glens Falls, emailed me. She said she and her sister had followed the blog for a while, and that she loved the photos of Frieda. She later added that one of her neighbors had told her they recognized Frieda from a photo I had posted on the blog. Stella said the photo reminded her of a dog she'd once had. Apparently Frieda looked very much like a dog her husband had bought from a backyard breeder in the Adirondacks and then trained as a guard dog. "My husband was old-school when it came to animals," she said, "kind of a jerk in some ways, I know." He had run an automotive repair shop and would buy dogs from this breeder and keep them in a kennel behind his garage. At the end of the workday, he would lock the gates and open the kennel and the dogs would patrol all night, keeping kids and thieves out. In the morning, when he came to work, they'd go into their kennels, where they'd alternately sleep and pace all day.

Stella said he trained the dogs by letting them loose, and then he and some buddies would approach the fence from the other side, banging on it with sticks or pots and pans, and poking at the dogs through the links. The dogs would go crazy, throwing themselves at the fence. The men would further antagonize the dogs, flinging rocks over the fence or kicking at it. Rottweilers and German shepherds are notoriously territorial, and such training would, of course, raise their prey drive to dangerous and almost unmanageable levels. It would be the perfect way to make dogs from either of those breeds crazy or "mean" and is yet another example of how dogs are turned "vicious" so easily by vicious people.

I drove out to see Stella. The house and street had seen better times. She lived in a small wooden bungalow a few miles from a large shopping mall on a street pockmarked with shuttered businesses and shops, most of the houses in need of paint and repair.

Stella was a large, middle-aged woman, a chain-smoker. She had brown hair and was wearing jeans and a sweatshirt. Her two small Chihuahuas barked continuously. She had worked at a nearby paper mill for fifteen years and had then been laid off. She was hoping to go back. "Part-time, no benefits. You know the story." I had indeed heard it before.

Like a lot of working-class women upstate, she wasn't all that crazy about men or life, but it was clear that she adored her dogs. She said you'd have to shoot her to get her to marry again, but she was thinking of getting another dog. They were small, and she had the room. She was almost always watching them, talking to them. Her husband, she told me, had died a few years earlier of a massive heart attack, right there in the driveway.

The auto body shop was behind the house, and I could see the kennel, now empty. Stella showed me photos of her old dog—there was no question it was Frieda, from the coloring and markings to the small distinctive growth near her eye.

"We called her Brownie," she said, smiling. "What else would you call her?"

I asked her to tell me Brownie's story.

Her husband had been a hard worker, she told me, and he was not sentimental about dogs. They were for work, he said, and you didn't need to coddle them. After the shop had been robbed three different times over a few months, he had asked a friend who was a policemen for the name of a breeder of guard dogs.

Stella went to a desk and brought me a letter on printed stationery and a receipt with the name of the kennel. It was in Warrensburg, a town in the Adirondacks about fifteen miles northwest of Glens Falls.

"I didn't like the guard dog idea," Stella said. "Seemed cruel to leave them outside like that. But Steve said that's what they were bred for, they didn't know the difference. These dogs were not pets, he said." Steve worked six days a week, fifty or sixty hours, Stella told me, and he wasn't about to see some neighborhood kids get rich off his blood and sweat.

She stopped to light up a Marlboro, and I started coughing. I hadn't been in a smoke-filled room for the longest time, and I was having trouble breathing. "Sorry," she said, going over to open a window. Her two small brown dogs were barking at me nonstop. Stella came on a bit rough at first, and it was clear that life was not easy for her, but I liked her. I had the sense that dogs were very important to her, that treating them well was important, and that she felt bad about Frieda. I think she had called me to clear her conscience a bit, and also to reassure herself that things had turned out okay for the dog she called Brownie.

She sat back on the sofa, the two dogs jumping up and crawling into her lap, where they growled and barked at me until she shushed them.

It was in the fall, she remembered, when she and Steve drove up to Warrensburg. The "breeder" lived in a double-wide trailer. Three dogs rushed the car, and they couldn't get out until their owner stuck his head out of the trailer, called them off, and locked them in the kennel. They were all rottweiler-shepherd mixes, Stella remembered, and they were serious about not letting her and Steve out of the car.

The breeder agreed to show them the puppies, then five weeks old. They were taken out back, to a shed surrounded by a rusty chain-link fence. "It was a dirty, foul-smelling place," she said, with six or seven puppies lying in mud and feces. The mother was in a separate kennel.

"It kind of tore me up to see them," she said. "You definitely wanted to bring one of them home, get them out of there."

Steve picked out one of the females, paid the man $50, and brought the dog home. Steve took her right out to the fenced-in yard. Stella said Brownie never came into the house, not once. Her husband built her a makeshift kennel out of some wire fencing he got at the hardware store.

"She has to get used to being alone," Steve told Stella, forbidding her to visit Brownie or give her treats or toys. She was going to be a guard dog, he said. She wasn't supposed to like people. She was supposed to hate and fear them and keep them away.

Steve kept some dry kibble in the shop and fed the dog twice a day.

"I have to confess that I did visit Brownie, when Steve wasn't looking or was away," Stella said. "I would bring her some biscuits and throw them over the fence. She never barked at me—she would always look at me and wag her tail." Stella explained how she would throw blankets over the fence in the winter, and how she got a soft dog bed, since Brownie had been sleeping on concrete.

"Brownie broke my heart," she said. "She was sweet, I think, underneath."

I could see this was difficult for her. "I've read a couple of your books," she said. "My mom gave one to me. I just feel bad about Brownie . . ."

Brownie was a good guard dog, she recalled. The break-ins stopped. Stella said nobody broke into the yard—not once—in the time Brownie was patrolling. The teasing from the neighborhood kids didn't stop, though. They would come by the fence and throw sticks and pebbles at her, and once Stella caught them tossing burning rags at Brownie, who would fling herself at the fence again and again, sometimes cutting her forelegs, snout, and paws.

Steve didn't believe in taking dogs to the vet, so Stella would go and bandage Brownie's scrapes. "She was very gentle with me—I was the only one who could touch her," she said. "But I was never afraid of her. I knew that look she gave me, it was full of love. And I always thought she was asking me to take care of her, bring her inside, out of the rain."

One night, at three in the morning, Brownie started barking. She barked so loud and so urgently that Steve grabbed his rifle and ran outside in his shorts. Stella followed. They had never heard this loud kind of a bark before; it was different, not something you could ignore.

"We ran outside, got to the shop, and opened the fence, and then we smelled the smoke. Steve looked up and yelled, 'Hey, go call the fire department. The neighbors' house is on fire.' We saw that it was the house two doors down, the third floor was in flames, and we knew there were a bunch of kids in that house, and we ran over there and started screaming, 'Get out, get out.'"

Stella stopped to light a fresh cigarette, and her dogs remained quiet. I could hear the clock on the table ticking while Stella, emotional now, gathered herself.

"Now, the neighbors heard us, and everybody was rushing out in the street, and then we heard the sirens and the family came rushing out with their four kids. All of them got out, all of them. Because of that dog, because of Brownie. She got them up."

The fire department wanted to give Brownie an award, Stella said, but Steve wouldn't hear of it. He was nervous, she thought, because of where the dog came from and how she lived. And maybe, she thought, he didn't want to have to think about her outdoors in a kennel, even in the frigid winters of upstate New York.

Steve was a good man in many ways, according to Stella, but when it came to dogs, he just had a blind spot. He could be cold. He was old-school, as she put it. When Brownie saved those kids, she said, she hoped he would relent, let the dog into the house on cold nights, let Stella play with her and take her for walks.

But he wouldn't. He said it would ruin her as a guard dog. She had to be out in the kennel twenty-four/seven and not bond with people. That's what the breeder had said makes a good guard dog.

Brownie was out in the kennel for two or three years. Then she got past the fence—she had dug a huge secret tunnel in a junk-filled corner, like some inmate in a prison movie—and was gone for five days. Stella said she went looking for Brownie, put up posters, called the police. But nobody saw her. Then, on the fifth day, Brownie came crawling back, exhausted, hungry, and all scratched up. Over the next few weeks, it became clear that she was pregnant. She started growing teats and a belly and eating funny.

Stella took a puff on her cigarette, cooed at one of her dogs.

"Steve was angry," she told me. "He kept railing on that she was ruined now, would be no good. He didn't want puppies, and didn't want to pay for vet bills. I was afraid he would give her away or worse."

Steve came into the house one night and said Brownie was gone, but he wouldn't say where she was. He said he had given her away. Stella said she didn't believe him, but he wouldn't talk about it.

A year or so later, when he was buzzed on some beer, she overheard him talking to one of his buddies in the shop office.

What Steve did, she learned, was drive the pregnant Brownie to the southern tier of the Adirondacks, about ten miles to the north, in the middle of the winter. He let her out of the car and drove off.

"It tears me up still," Stella says, "it just pulls my heart out. She was a good dog. A sweet dog at heart. They made her crazy. Then she was dumped out in the woods."

It was then that I understood why Stella had invited me out to her house.

"Do you think I could see Brownie again, just one more time?"

I said no, I thought not, not for a while. I said it might be confusing for the dog. It was certain that Brownie and Frieda were one and the same, and I was glad I had come. Now I understood more about why Frieda was the way she was, something we rarely get to learn about our dogs. Stella said it might help her get rid of some of the guilt if she saw Brownie was in a new home, and that she was okay.

I said I'd think it over.

Later, I wondered why I'd been so quick to say no to Stella's wish to meet Frieda again.

I thought it might be because I felt a lot of anger in that house. I understood a bit of Stella's life, the pickle she was in. But still, she had stood by for all of that, stayed with this man.

She had told me about the night Steve took Frieda out in the car and then, an hour later, came back without her. She knew very well what had happened. Still, it is easy to judge other people, and I was working hard not to do it. Stella was clearly a good person who'd been in a bad situation. She'd done what she could, like most people. It was not for me to judge her. There was too much of that among people involved with animals, too much self-righteousness. I had made plenty of mistakes myself, and I suspect some were a lot bigger than hers.

"I cried myself to sleep that night," Stella told me, "and a lot of nights, but the way things were, you couldn't say anything, really. Not in my life."

I thanked Stella for contacting me and told her that I understood that doing so could not have been easy. I said we all do what we have to do to survive in life, and we all make our own decisions and have to live by them. My life with animals, I said, was not about judging or hating people.

"What if I called you in a few months," I offered, "and we could talk again about your meeting Frieda?" It wouldn't be for a while, I went on to explain, as Frieda was not ready. Frankly, I wasn't sure she would ever be ready for that. But it seemed like the right thing to leave the door open.

"I would be so grateful for that," said Stella. "It's why I emailed you. It would do more for me than you know."

The truth is, I was grateful to Stella. She hadn't had to contact me or open up to me the way she had. Her guilt and regret were evident. And I had learned some critically important things about Frieda. Perhaps this was why she was so overstimulated by strangers and why she was so territorial.

She had been trained as a guard dog. That was her work. No wonder she was so intense about keeping people away from doorways and fences. And keeping me away from Maria. I thought about the kids who'd tormented her with sticks and rocks, and Steve, who, with his friends, aroused her and brought up all that prey drive, and then dumped her out in the Adirondacks to fend for herself, which, apparently, she'd done.

I don't ever like to see my dogs as abused or as "rescued." Those are terms human beings use to project our own needs onto animals. Dogs are adaptable, retrainable. They do not see themselves as piteous or mistreated. They move on. If Frieda was to survive in my new life with Maria, that was what we had to do with her: move on.

Now I had some ideas about how to do it.

Chapter Twelve

Dreams *Do* Come True

In my dream, I was driving my daughter and her friends to school. I got up early, went to the kitchen, prepared a lunch for Emma—peanut butter and jelly, I think, with an apple and a cookie. I walked out to the garage, waved to the stream of neighbors headed for the train, warmed up the big blue minivan. Three days a week, I was the car-pool driver, scooting around my affluent suburban town to pick up three other kids, all girls, whose moods seemed as fluid as the weather.

I woke up with a fluttering heart. I don't know to this day if this was a memory dream or a nightmare. I remember looking out the window, seeing the donkeys, glancing at the foot of the bed, seeing Lenore, aware of the misty mountains in the distance, and this beautiful and loving human being next to me.

Nothing in my dream had survived. My daughter lived far away in Brooklyn and found the country primitive and dull. There was no affluent town, no garage, no neighbors streaming by, no minivan. My other world has vanished.

In her own way, in a different context, Maria would often have the same kind of dream.

We were all—Frieda included—inhabitants of a murky, ill-defined world. I loved the farm, but much of my life—the professional part in New York City, the married home owner in the suburbs part, the child-rearing part—had broken off like a glacier. I'd never consciously intended for the farm to be my whole existence, for every friend and much of the family who had shaped my adult life to simply vanish.

I'd never thought that I would need, at age sixty-one, to learn how to open a bank account, figure out insurance policies, deal with utilities, budget money, split assets, grasp the intricate nature of royalties and the very uncertain financial life of a writer.

I had always passed that stuff on and avoided it. Now I was drowning in bills, paperwork, and terror.

One night I got an email from Anne, a gentle, soft-voiced woman who had been helping to restore the gardens on the farm. She worked quietly with her beloved flowers, and I had barely spoken with her, she was so shy and I was so distracted.

"You look like you need help," the email said, adding that she was a bookkeeper. Although I hardly knew her, I wrote back, "Yes, I need help," and so began one of the most remarkable and important friendships in my life.

She was staggered by the financial mess she found. It took her a few weeks to figure it all out. One problem was that I had been double-paying the mortgage and the auto and home insurance bills. I was so terrified by paperwork and the foot-high stack of bills that I sent a check when the payment was due, and then sent another check when the receipt arrived. I had no local bank account and was unaware of online banking. (I was too important a creative person to bother with that stuff, you see.)

When I returned from a book tour in the Midwest, Maria picked me up at the Albany airport. We walked into the house, and I saw that the light in my home office was on. It was Anne, at my computer, a huge stack of bills and papers by her side, and my bank account called up on the screen.

She turned to me and said, without preamble, "Hi, Jon. It's time to panic."

That was all I needed to hear, because I was completely wired for panic. Maria, horrified by the look on my face, tried to protect me. "Surely it's not that bad," she said.

I loved her for that, for trying to shield me from this quiet bookkeeper with long braids who worked in bare feet.

"I'm not going to coddle him," Anne said. So it was.

Anne helped save me that winter, organizing my bills and finances, handling my taxes, navigating the new world of online banking, collecting the mounds of receipts and paperwork. Sorting through it all with Anne, I thought the top of my head was going to come off. And it did.

That winter, I was nearly devoured by panic, and so was Maria.

It's not real, we would tell each other as the dark approached and the gloom deepened. The panic isn't real.

Maybe so. But without it, what's left?

Maria was not having an easier time of it. She was literally penniless. Like me, she had no real idea how to live in the world, and no confidence that she could do it even if she learned.

Like me, she wrestled daily with panic and confusion. She felt awash in guilt and shame. We were isolated. Frieda moved like a ghost between us, the spirit in the barn, a reminder of work not yet done.

Dogs are sensitive, Frieda especially so, and she was uneasy and anxious. It wasn't clear what her future was either, and she too had no idea how to live in the world. Her life had just been broken apart, and she had so many new things to learn, just like Maria and I did. Three lost souls trying to stay afloat. "At your age, most decisions should be made," one very serious analyst told me. "Yours are just beginning."

Yes, this was so. It was not clear what would happen to the three of us. Would we become a family or head back out into the world, looking to rebuild our fragmented lives in other places with other people?

Frieda's life was shrinking. A two-room apartment in Granville, a small barn on the farm. She had no idea where she lived anymore, or what her purpose was. The man she was trying to keep away was there all the time, bringing her food. Maria left her to spend nights somewhere else. Dogs that should be run off were in her face every morning, and animals that should be run down or hunted were all around her, and she couldn't chase them or hunt them. Life was topsy-turvy.

During that rip-roaring, old-fashioned upstate winter, we were freezing all the time. Years ago, I had gotten frostbite during some ill-considered winter lambing, and my fingers and toes ached in the cold. Our noses were always running, our bones chilled. We were lonely and out of our minds with anxiety. We ran to therapists, counselors, consulted self-help books on codependence and panic attacks, listened to inspirational tapes, read Rumi and Mary Oliver poems to each other. We cried, held hands, walked in the snow, hung on to each other.

As I lay awake one night, I realized that we needed to change the scene; we needed to get out of Bedlam for at least a few days. Maria and I needed some perspective, some time together away from the site of anguish and anxiety. My therapist had suggested a trip to someplace warm. "I can't afford it," I'd said. "You can't afford not to," she'd replied.

I got up, Googled a travel agent in Albany, left a message for her. "Hey," I said, "my name is Jon Katz. I need to book a trip right away to someplace warm. An easy trip. For two. To Disney World."

Why did I choose Disney World? I have always loved Disney World. I took my daughter, Emma, there when she was eighteen months old, and I've loved it ever since. It's warm and cheerful, and the people there know what they are doing when it comes to hospitality and entertainment.

I've always loved the Polynesian Village and its cheesy hula-hula ambience and its closeness to the Magic Kingdom. Disney created an alternate universe, a safe respite from the pressures of the outside world.

Like a lot of boomers, I grew up a Disney kid. Walt Disney reached into my life and comforted me, tapping into my imagination. As a media critic, I was always fascinated by Disney's obsession with technology, and the way it played itself out in the rides, architecture, and ethos of Disney World. In fact, I'd been working on a book about Disney and his intense relationship with technology when life intervened, and I got a border collie named Orson and wrote my first book about dogs, *A Dog Year*.

Maria was shocked by my plan. She couldn't afford a vacation, she said, and why Disney World? Wasn't it for kids? Wasn't it a bit tacky? Why not someplace cheaper, quieter, nearer?

But Maria, like me, was hanging on by her fingernails. She didn't have the stomach for arguing, not if the place was warm. And she saw that I loved Disney World, was fascinated by it, felt at home there.

So I just booked the tickets, after negotiations and discussions about room views, meal plans, and theme park passes. The recession was in full force, and Disney was in an accommodating mood. I got a nice room at the Polynesian (no water view) with breakfast and lunch thrown in. A cheap flight from Albany to Orlando and back. The whole jaunt cost less than $3,000. No, I couldn't afford it, but the therapist was right. We called a kennel, made reservations for Frieda and my dogs, and found a friend to stay at the farm.

A week later, we were on a plane to Orlando.

The morning we left, it was seventeen degrees. We drove to the Albany airport and parked the car in the long-term lot. All the way in, Maria was dubious. "Are we really going to Disney World?" she kept asking. "I know, I know," I said. "It isn't cool. It isn't New Mexico or the Caribbean. It's Mickey Mouse."

But when we stepped off the plane and onto Disney's

"Magical Express" bus, Maria turned to me, beaming. "We are warm," she said. "We are warm." It was sunny and bright. And people were nice to us. More people said hello to us on the bus than had spoken to us for weeks.

The bus driver, an elderly Cuban refugee, asked where we were from, and I told him we were from upstate New York and were on our first trip together as a couple. He reached down, handed me a yellow paper flower to give to Maria, and smiled.

"Wow," Maria said, beaming. "He approves of us."

He was the first person to do so, as near as we could tell. We appreciated it. We appreciated being warm. We loved all the Hawaiian mumbo jumbo (everybody says "aloha" there), the palm trees, the water boats.

We loved the cereal, fruit, and bagel bar, open all day for us. We took our shoes off and ran to the pool.

Then we got dressed and took the ferry over to the Magic Kingdom, listening to all the whistles, rushing past the "lagoons," soaking up the energy of all the happy kids and beaming parents. At Disney, I remembered, all the boats and trains in were filled with happy people. On the way back, they were all broke and exhausted.

We were deliriously happy. We flashed our passes and were swept into the Magic Kingdom along with all of the crowds. I knew this place well, where all the good rides and short lines were. Disney World requires considerable strategizing. I was good at it.

For me, the chance to bring Maria to this oddly familiar place, to show it to her, affirmed us as a couple. We talked and talked—on the ferry, on the monorail. We laughed on the rides, yakked through dinner, slept in each other's arms.

Maria would never have gone to Disney World by herself, and it was not the sort of thing she'd ever expected anyone else to arrange for her. We were surrounded by the best parts of the genial American spirit. People joked with us on the paths, in the pool, said hello, beamed when we told them our story, were happy for us, wished us well. A tonic, all of it, the warmth, the cheerfulness, the healthy dose of light and color and life.

I took Maria to Pirates of the Caribbean, then the Haunted Mansion, then the splash ride. If Disney World wasn't really an artist's first choice among travel destinations, it did bring out the kid in her. I began to see a part of Maria I had not seen before. She laughed all day, seemed to soak up the warmth and the food and the comfort. I saw that she was deprived, and was beginning to feel nourished. I saw how happy she was to get away from the sadness and misery of the last few years. I saw what an amazingly good time we were having together, how much we connected, how comfortable we were with each other. And I realized it wasn't just Disney World that made both of us happy. It was simply being together.

Maria, I realized, was a great sport. She went on all the dumb rides and loved Splash Mountain, shrieking like a little kid as we caromed through the water. On that ride, I watched her smile and laugh and I understood that I was beginning to learn what love was. Maria had never wanted to go to Disney World; she would have probably rather gone to New Mexico, walked through the desert, browsed some classy art galleries.

Maria loved Disney World because I loved Disney World, the same way I was coming to love secondhand clothing stores, Indian music, and brussels sprouts. We each loved what the other loved, with an open heart and soul. Over time, I came to see, we loved almost everything we did together, because we were doing it together. This kind of selflessness was new to me, and I was grateful to learn it and live it. What, I asked myself, is love, really? I thought about that on that ride, and as we dried ourselves off and looked for popcorn. It is about the other, I decided, not the self.

In Downtown Disney, I sat on a bench while Maria went into a shop to buy presents for her nieces and nephew. I was sitting next to a man in an Ohio State University Buckeyes T-shirt and a battered U.S. Navy cap. He was a large man with a ruddy face and a warm and generous smile. He had, as I suspected, served in Vietnam, and was now retired.

We got to talking. He said his name was Jim and that he was from Dayton. He had just remarried. Cathy, his new wife, was in the same shop as Maria. His first wife had died of cancer. His kids were having trouble with his moving on, and I nodded in understanding. He had brought Cathy to Disney World, to celebrate their new life.

We were both taking in the stream of people pushing toward the giant restaurants and shops, the kids in strollers, the kids in hats, with balloons, holding bags, the tired moms and dads.

We talked about marrying again, and the challenges and joys of it. I said Maria was my girlfriend and that I hoped she would marry me one day, someday soon, as I was already rounding sixty. He roared with laughter.

"Yeah," he said, "they give you all these warnings, like second marriage is a disease, and you have to be careful about this and that. But at my age, I don't worry about that so much. You have to take some chances. The people I know who are so careful don't have much fun."

Then he surprised me. He leaned toward me, took his cap off, and put his hand on my shoulder, and he looked me straight in the eye. His eyes were commanding and blue and very confident.

"Don't listen to people who have all these reasons not to be happy. To be in love at our age is a miracle, a gift straight from God, the most important thing in the world. Don't blow it."

Chapter Thirteen

"She Saved Our Lives"

Yༀou have to know a dog to train a dog, and when we returned from Disney World, momentarily warm and revived, I was prepared to focus more on Frieda. Spring was slow in coming, but I could see beyond the bleak winter, and my spirits were improving. Moods affect training. If you're up and ready, chances are the dog will be too.

Maria and I were growing ever closer, and now I needed to help Frieda move along with us, or risk her getting left behind.

The first morning back, after Maria had gone to work, I went to the studio barn to give Frieda some beef jerky and try to put a leash on her. She growled, then snapped at me, narrowly missing my hand. It wasn't a bite, but it wasn't friendly.

Frieda was powerful, frightening, and, in many ways, an

out-of-control dog. But I was grateful to her for loving and protecting Maria through difficult times. That was worth a lot to me, to both of us. She deserved a good and safe life. It was my job to give it to her. But she was not easy. She had lived in a solitary world of arousal and lack of attention, doing what very few dogs in America ever get to do: survive by her instincts. Some of her formative experiences harkened back to the early days of dogs and the wolves from which they are descended: hunting for her own food, finding her own shelter, making her own way in the world.

I think training a dog is ultimately a mental process and that humans are smarter than dogs, for all we love to emotionalize and anthropomorphize them. It's our job to figure them out, not the other way around. We have the tools to do that, even if they have the instincts. People are always telling me what their dogs are thinking, but when it comes to training, I've learned that it's more important to understand what I am thinking.

I needed to know Frieda; through that, I might be able to train her. People mostly just want their dogs to be housebroken and not eat their possessions or chew up the furniture. But I think dogs need a lot more than that to live in our world.

They need to understand the boundaries of our difficult world, so that we can accept them and they can coexist with us safely. I wanted Frieda to obey me, for sure, but more than that, her life with us depended on her learning how to get along with us and the other dogs and animals on the farm. There was no training theory I knew of that covered that.

I had finally called Stella, Frieda's former owner, and told her I wanted to bring Frieda out to South Glens Falls the following day. She said she had decided that she wasn't sure she wanted to see Frieda after all, that it might be too hard for her. She felt bad, but she said I was welcome to come by anyway. She told me to knock on her door. If she was home, she might say hello.

I realized that when I had gone to see Stella, I'd been angered by the story she'd told me. It seemed to me she was the one person who might have helped Frieda, stopped her from being abandoned in the forest while pregnant. But after I thought it through, that response seemed unfair. She obviously felt awful about what had happened. I had seen so much anger in purported animal advocates, so much judging, self-righteousness, and accusation. I had become allergic to that. I didn't want that to be part of *my* life with animals. It might be healing for her to see Frieda, and what benefit would come from trying to stop that?

So the next morning, Maria and I got Frieda into the car, and I drove with Frieda to South Glens Falls to revisit the site of her guard dog days. Maria and I had agreed that she should stay home. Her presence might distract Frieda or trigger her protective instincts. Also, Maria wasn't sure she could handle seeing the place where Frieda had endured such rough treatment. Because Frieda would still not allow me to leash her, Maria had to do it before we set off.

Frieda hopped up into the rear of my car without complaint, and we drove the fifteen miles to South Glens Falls. My plan was to visit the auto body shop and then, later, to go to the area of the Adirondacks where Frieda had been dumped, to see what I could learn from her behavior and demeanor.

We pulled up to Stella's house a little after nine A.M. There was a car in the driveway, and I saw the curtains shift. Somebody was home. Stella had told me I could walk around if she wasn't home. I heard barking. I remembered her two little dogs. Frieda wasn't going in there. I walked around to the side of the house and saw the auto body shop Stella's husband had run, now shuttered.

This was one of those upstate quasi-urban neighborhoods, near a city but with a country feel—gardens, no sidewalks, lots of barking dogs. The area had seen better days. Even on the poorest upstate streets, there was little litter, but lots of debris in the yards—old cars, abandoned mowers and auto parts, rusting barbecue grills. There was a shuttered corner store a block down the road, and an abandoned pizza place.

Before me was the familiar stucco garage and shed, with the motor vehicle inspection stickers. The work area was surrounded by a rusting chain-link fence, the front gates open. The windows of the shop were broken, and there were cans and bottles around. It looked completely forgotten.

I went to the back of the car and opened the gate; Frieda was sitting there, looking at me. No growling or staring this time; she just seemed nervous. I reached in, got the end of the leash, called her, and she jumped out, looked around. I hadn't seen this Frieda before: her tail was down, her ears were back, and she crouched close to the ground.

She gazed up at me. While I am wary of putting my words in a dog's head, her expression definitely seemed to say, "Get me out of here." She leaned close to me, almost brushing against me, and we walked through the open gate, into the yard. There were still three or four trucks and some old cars against the fence in the rear.

I headed there. As we rounded the corner, I saw a kennel, about twelve by six feet, a good size, with a small wooden doghouse—now falling apart—at one end. That would have been Frieda's kennel, and her "shelter." A rough place to spend an upstate winter, I thought.

Frieda took it in, surveying it from one end to the other, raising her nose in the air. She was subdued. She had lost her swagger; her head was lowered. She had a hangdog look.

Viewing the scene, I could see how they had used her. With the main gate closed, Frieda could be left out at night to patrol the chain-link fence, which covered about a quarter acre. She could easily have watched an area that size, and I could see that no intruder would have stood a chance if she was there.

As we walked back to the kennel, Frieda's tail was so low it was almost dragging on the ground. She stopped when we got to the kennel gate, and I didn't open it. Who really knows, I wondered, what a dog thinks? She was different, for sure, but I didn't know how much she remembered, or what her instincts were telling her. She surely had lost her aggressive stance, her alertness. She was leaning into me, staying close, no pulling on the leash.

I took her around the perimeter, stepping over rusted tail-pipes and beer cans. As we got near the fence, Frieda stiffened, barked, and lunged. I saw a cat on the other side of the chain link vanish. I understood, standing on that concrete, near that fence, why Frieda was so intense about boundaries. This was what she had learned to do. Keep the world out. This was what she was still trying to do. The boundary was clear: the fence. And a protective dog like Frieda, excited by banging on the other side, would have patrolled this territory very aggressively. Her prey drive would have been cranked up every time a bicycle or a car or group of kids went by. And I had seen plenty of upstate kids taunt dogs on leashes and behind fences. It happened to mine all the time, and they were not nearly as territorial as Frieda.

She was becoming increasingly tense inside the fence. She wasn't sure what to do, I could see that, but she was staying close to me, as if I were better than the alternative. And I imagined I was. The Beef Jerky Campaign was a whole lot more appealing than this job.

We stood for a while by the fence, then walked out the front gates and down the street a ways. Frieda was eager to go.

We made our way up the street, down the street, and then around the corner. We strolled for about half an hour. I noticed that Frieda was walking easily by my side, in step, as if she had been trained. I guessed the problem we'd had at the studio barn was my reaching for her and entering her space, not really walking with her.

As we headed back toward the auto body shop and Stella's house, I saw a woman pulling some weeds from a tiny garden in the front of her home. I started to cross to the other side of the street, not wanting to startle her with Frieda's barking. I held the leash tightly, but to my surprise, Frieda didn't bark or growl. She looked lighter, relieved. The woman was watching us intently. As we got close, she rose to her feet, smiled, and walked toward us. Frieda growled, letting out a low rumble, then went silent.

"I'm not sure she's friendly," I said apologetically.

The woman smiled at Frieda. "Oh, I know her," she said. "My boys used to call her Goldie. That's not her name, I know they called her Brownie, but it's the name we used." She looked right at Frieda and held her hand out, and Frieda trotted over to her and put her head in the woman's hand. She was not demonstrative, was not jumping up or wagging her tail, just at ease. Frieda was not a cuddly dog. She never let anyone but Maria touch her. In fact, I had never seen her be this friendly to anyone but Maria.

I was startled by what happened next; it didn't in any way fit with my understanding of Frieda, incomplete as that was.

The woman dropped down to her knees in front of Frieda, who put her head right on the woman's chest as she spoke softly to her, scratching her ears and rubbing the sides of her head. Then, to my surprise, the woman kissed Frieda right on the nose.

"I'm not sure she's safe around people, being touched like that," I stammered, starting to pull back on the leash.

"She's okay with me," she said, unfazed. "I know this dog."

"Hey, Goldie," she said, talking to her as if she were the sweetest little puppy in the world. As if she were Lenore.

She held up her hand, then ran into the house and emerged with a piece of raw hamburger and gave it to Frieda, whose tail was now wagging. Frieda swallowed it right down, then sat there eagerly, awaiting more.

The woman's eyes were moist. I saw it before I understood it. She and Frieda had a very powerful connection. They knew and trusted each other. It didn't fit with what I knew of Frieda's history, unless . . .

"This was the house with the fire, right?"

I introduced myself. She said her name was Cheryl. She was dabbing at her eyes with a handkerchief, looking at Frieda, unable to take her eyes off the dog. "She saved our lives," she said. "My kids are in school now, all four of them, and none of them would be alive if not for her. If not for Goldie."

It was her son Sean who'd named the dog Goldie, she said, probably after his goldfish. Frieda's coloring was brown and black; she was anything but gold. Cheryl bit her lip as I asked her about that night.

She said Goldie had become a favorite target for neighborhood kids. They tossed firecrackers over the fence, banged on it with pots and pans, raked sticks along the wire mesh. They jumped against the fence and would start to climb it to see how fast Goldie could get out and charge. If they reached the top—higher than she could leap—they'd toss rocks down at her.

Cheryl told me that her husband used to go out and chase the kids away, but he couldn't be there all the time. It was awful, she said, to think of the dog lying out there in the rain and snow and cold.

It was her son Sean who first brought food to the dog. He would toss her leftover meat from dinner, and then he started to hold it through the chain link. Over time, Cheryl told me, Goldie would come up and take it without barking at Sean, but he was the only one. Goldie wouldn't let any other person do it.

Cheryl had tried talking to Stella about the poor dog, but there was nothing she could do. If you knew Steve, Cheryl said, you knew that that was so.

Once, her husband was driving by and saw Steve whaling on the dog with a piece of aluminum fender. He pulled over to confront him. But Steve only told him to mind his own business. He said that Goldie was a guard dog and that she needed to be afraid of people, suspicious of them; otherwise she wouldn't keep them out. She wasn't a pet. He had bought her as a guard dog and that was what he wanted her to do. Liking people was not part of a guard dog's life.

But Sean didn't care about that argument. He went to see her every day, bought dog biscuits with his allowance, wrapped meat and bread and leftovers in napkins and plastic wrap and carried them over. He had to be careful not to let Steve see, as he would get furious and chase him away, and maybe, Sean worried, whale on Frieda. So he was careful, usually going at night when Stella and her husband were too wasted to hear anything or care.

Cheryl told me some more about what she saw, what Sean saw, and what the neighbors saw and heard. Honestly, some of it was pretty ugly—kicks, torment from kids passing by, exposure to heat, ice, bitter cold, rain, bugs, and sores. Maria had been right not to come. Frieda is in a different place now. That life is no longer her reality.

Sean and Goldie got closer and closer, but the taunting and mistreatment went on, and they could all see and hear that. Cheryl said she eventually called Glens Falls Animal Control and asked the workers there if it was legal to treat a dog this way. Stella's husband was right, they said. If the dog had food and shelter and water, there was nothing they could do. If she could get a photo of him beating the dog, then that might be something they could pursue. But even then, it was a misdemeanor ticket, and he might just beat the dog worse if he got in trouble over her. It often happened that way.

Cheryl said that one day Goldie disappeared. Her family cheered and prayed that she had found a different home. They were all sad when they got up one morning and heard the barking from the auto body shop. Goldie had returned.

"Why didn't she run away?" asked Cheryl. "Why didn't she just keep going? But," she added, "thank God she did come back."

"It's the way of dogs," I said. "Loyal beyond reason sometimes, slaves to what they know."

Cheryl stopped talking for a moment and closed her eyes. She reached down and patted Frieda, who lay by her feet, looking up at her, still, calm, at ease.

Cheryl resumed her story and spoke about the night she heard Goldie barking while the rest of the family was asleep. It was an unusual bark, Cheryl said, not Goldie's typical frantic, aggressive racket. The barking sounded alarmed, urgent. Something was wrong.

"My husband and I were asleep. Four kids in the house, two in a downstairs bedroom, two in a makeshift bedroom in the attic. It's a small house and we were meaning to add on, but my husband lost his job, so we had to wait."

She got up, put her bathrobe on while the barking got louder. She went downstairs—the auto body shop was just a couple of doors down—and before she reached the bottom of the stairs, she smelled the smoke pouring out from the rear of the house where the electric box was, and she knew that was what Goldie was barking at, knew exactly what was wrong. She screamed for her husband to get the kids out, grabbed the cellphone, called 911. She remembers that she and her husband flew upstairs and literally threw the two boys—Sean and his brother—out the front window and onto the porch roof just below.

The two girls downstairs got out right away—they had done plenty of fire drills. The volunteers were there in minutes, and by that time, the smoke and flames were so thick, they said, nobody could have gotten out. The top two floors were destroyed, but Cheryl and her husband had good insurance, and they were able to rebuild. They went to stay with Cheryl's mother in Fort Edward while the new house was under construction.

By the time they moved back, she said, Goldie was gone, and nobody would say what had happened to her.

"That night, when we got out of the house, and the trucks were here, we were all standing on the street, in our robes, watching our house burn. We could have sat in the rescue truck to be warm, but we wanted to see everything. We couldn't believe it. My younger son started whining about his computer, and I remember grabbing him and saying, 'Don't you dare complain about a thing. Jesus sent that dog here to protect us, and she did, and let's all go over there and thank her,' and we walked right down the street—the firemen chasing after us with blankets—and we marched right up to the fence. Goldie had been barking like crazy at the fire trucks, but when she saw Sean, she just lay down on the ground, and she whimpered a bit. I'll never forget that. You will never tell me anything but that this dog is an angel sent to save my family. Houses don't matter, money doesn't matter when you have your life, and your children have their lives."

It was quiet for a minute. I was near tears. It was such a powerful story. I didn't know if Frieda had consciously decided to save their lives or not, but what did it matter? How wondrous is the history of dogs, and the story of their relationship with people. How much comfort have dogs provided, how many lives saved by barks and growls and alarms coming from their exquisitely sensitive canine consciousness? Instinctively, I reached down to pet Frieda, to stroke her head. She growled and snapped at my hand, and I pulled it back. I just smiled at her.

As I was saying goodbye, I gave Cheryl my phone number and invited her to come to the farm and see Frieda anytime she wanted. She said she hoped the dog was in a good place, warm and safe and loved. She deserved that. I assured her that she was.

She gave "Goldie" a final hug.

As we began to walk away from her house, two bicycles came around the corner and I held tight to Frieda, expecting her to growl, but she didn't. One of the bikes veered away, and the other pulled up. A gangly adolescent boy hopped off and walked right up to Frieda without a moment's hesitation.

"Wait," I said, "she may not be friendly."

"She's friendly to me," he said. And I knew it was Sean.

Frieda let out a little whine, but of joy, not warning, and rolled over onto her side, wagging her tail, and Sean leaned over her, giving her a long tight hug and then scratching her belly. He had no fear of her at all.

Children and dogs never forget each other; they form bonds that are both unforgettable and unbreakable. That was what I was seeing: a connection between a child and this wild creature that simply defied explanation or understanding. They had, in their own ways, saved each other. Sean had put into Frieda's neglected consciousness the notion of a trustworthy human being and kept that instinct alive. Frieda had saved the boy's life in return.

So I saw this other side of Frieda, the true side of a great dog.

After a few minutes, Sean nodded to me, got back on his bike, and rode home to his mom, who was watching us from down the block.

Frieda stood up and began walking beside me. I doubted that she and Sean would ever see each other again. Dogs have little use for sentimental notions of parting. They live mostly in the now. What they remember, I think, are the connections they make, the smells, feelings, sights, and sounds.

There was nothing especially emotional about Sean's meeting with Frieda, and after they said hello, both separated and went on with their lives. Sean didn't look back, and neither did Frieda. It was almost businesslike, but no less powerful for that.

I learned a number of things from our trip to South Glens Falls. Frieda took her work very seriously. You could connect with her, if the circumstances were right. To be honest, I was shocked by her ease with Sean and his mother. And a bit hurt. I had been with Frieda for months and had not broken through in that way. I asked myself what the message was, what the lesson was, but I didn't know. I could see that I had not connected with her as they had, and maybe that was something for me to think about.

More than ever, I knew that Frieda needed to be in our family. I turned to her on the sidewalk, on the way back to Stella's.

"Frieda," I said, "I'm committed to you. We'll work it out."

But she only looked at me and sniffed at the ground, uninterested in my ringing declarations.

As we approached my car, the door to Stella's house opened, and I could hear the two little dogs barking behind her. Frieda growled, stiffened, barked, perhaps at the dogs. This was so different than her meeting Cheryl or Sean, I thought. What does she remember?

Stella looked exhausted, or perhaps hungover. She was holding a lit cigarette in her right hand, down by her side.

"Hey, Brownie," she said. "I'm sorry. I hope you have a good life now. Maybe one day you'll forgive me."

And then she backed into the house and closed the door.

Brownie, Goldie, Frieda. This was a lot for one dog to process. She'd been a guard dog. She had connected to a young boy. She protected Maria. Now she was being asked to assume a new and completely different role, in many ways the most complex yet.

I wanted to explore the other Frieda, the Adirondack Frieda, next. It would complete the puzzle for me. Stella had given me the name of the breeder who'd sold her, and the shelter had told me where she had roamed after Stella's husband dumped her in the woods.

I wanted to get a feel for Frieda's life in the wild. Then I would know all I could know, maybe all I needed to know.

Frieda looked up at the doorway where Stella had vanished, tilting her ears as if she was trying to remember, and I heard a soft but determined growl.

"Let's get home, girl," I said.

Chapter Fourteen

Into the Wild

Our first stop was the breeder who'd sold Frieda to Steve. He had moved, but I found him through a simple website offering "Protection Dogs" for sale, and from the photos I understood that he specialized in rottweiler-shepherd mixes. The dogs ranged from $150 to $300, depending on age and breed.

The address I had was fifteen miles west of Blue Mountain Lake, the home of the Adirondack Museum. Cell and satellite signals were sporadic in the Adirondacks, so I had to stop two or three times before I could find the breeder's home.

My sense of the Adirondacks as a rough and remote place was reinforced when I pulled up to the breeder's address. He lived in a small split-level, gray with worn shingles and aluminum siding. An old car and two rusting pickups littered the yard by his garage. There was a small trailer behind the house and, beyond that, two or three old kennels, rusted and bent.

The kennels looked crowded, littered with junk. I could smell the feces across the road. This was what Frieda's birthplace had been like.

It was easy to recognize this place—and it was no surprise. It had all of the hallmarks of the backyard breeder. A slapdash kennel, dirty and crowded. And a breeder who didn't want to talk about his dogs. If there is one consistent hallmark of good dog breeders, it is an almost addictive desire to talk about their breeding programs and their dogs, and show them off. Good breeders have nothing to hide and are almost universally expansive about and proud of the work they do. I was sure this man's customers pulled up in pickups and just wanted dogs to guard their business equipment and storage facilities.

I saw four or five dogs running in one of the kennels; they appeared to be five or six months old. It was one of those drab Adirondack days, mist hanging over the hills, light and sun blocked by tall pines and peaks.

I looked at the house for a minute. A sign out front read, "Protection Dogs," just as the website had, and listed a phone number. I had sat there for a few minutes when a dark, heavyset man in jeans and a hooded sweatshirt came out and stared at me.

I looked at him, then got out of the car. He was wary, vigilant. He did not greet me or shake my hand. He was not welcoming in any way. He seemed secretive and hostile.

I told him I had a dog in my car that had probably come from his kennel, and he looked across the road and said, "Well, could be." Did I have any papers? he asked. I said no. I doubted there were very many "papers" associated with his dogs.

Did I have any problems with the dog? he asked. I said no, she had been somebody else's dog; she had been a guard dog. He nodded, said nothing.

I could see his suspicions growing as he stared at me. I suspected I didn't fit the usual profile. He said he didn't have any dogs for sale at the moment and didn't know when he might. That struck me as a lie. I had been a reporter for many years in big cities, and I knew I was looking at the kind of man the cops always called a "doubtful." They meant somebody who was sleazy, suspicious. Since he didn't know me, he was taking no chances.

My mind flashed back to Gretchen, Lenore's breeder, and how she'd invited me into her house for corn muffins and tea, insisted I meet each one of her breeding dogs, including Lenore's mom, spent an hour telling me about her breeding and temperament programs, and then put Lenore on my shoulder.

And finally, she'd insisted that I take a week or so to think about it.

This was a different world.

This man said he had no memory of Steve or any particular dog. He just bred them and sold them. He said he had to go. I was glad to leave. There was no reason for me to want to stay. I flirted briefly with the idea of offering to buy one or two of his puppies and getting them good homes. But I didn't; I just wanted to be gone. Frieda was quiet in the car, watching through the rear window.

As I pulled out, I wasn't even sure, at that moment, why I

had driven all the way out here, other than to fill in the circle that was Frieda's life. To see where she had come from, how she had lived.

The scene was depressing, and I knew the story all too well. I had seen what I needed to see, and when all was said and done, I had nothing to say to this man or to ask him. And I didn't really want to hear what he had to say to me. I knew what I needed to know. Now, more than ever, I was anxious to leave this doubtful man behind and explore the next chapter of Frieda's life in the Adirondacks. I was betting that it was better than this.

People have strong reactions to the Adirondacks. I know I do. I find it a lonely, broken, and beautiful place.

Some people are drawn to the quiet, shadowy, densely forested remoteness, the vast sense of wilderness. I prefer the open country, rolling hills and pastures. The Adirondacks have always had a haunting, slightly disturbing air for me. There are few people, no large communities. There is little work there anymore, and the once prosperous towns exist mostly to serve visitors and second-homers. Old sheds, buildings, burned-out and abandoned cabins, and incongruous split-levels dot the landscape. In between are the great lodges and old inns, many of them shuttered.

Then there are vast stretches of forest that feel like they can just swallow a person up. The sun rarely penetrates the thick pine canopy, and the mornings are often dark and misty.

This is the land of darkness, of shadows, the perfect place

to vanish beyond the consciousness of the so-called civilized world. In the Adirondacks, there is the sense of entering a different space, a wild space still. This is the wilderness that a pregnant Frieda had to face on her own.

There are more than six million acres in the vast Adirondack Park, few of them inhabited. None of the dogs I had ever owned would have survived there for a week. Driving and walking through the area, I imagined Frieda there. She was with me, sniffing the ground, uneasy.

I saw lots of structures that a dog could hole up in and take shelter: empty homes, vacant barns, lean-tos and sheds and caves, rock formations and fallen trees. Small game is plentiful for a hunting dog, and Frieda is definitely a hunter. As you move toward the southeast edge of the park, the area becomes more densely populated, especially heavily developed Lake George and the suburbs sprawling north of Glens Falls. Here are places for an enterprising dog to find food in the garbage, water in lakes and streams, friendly people, shelter. Every dog is different. Some breeds would simply go to a home and try to make contact with the human beings there, associating them with food.

Some dogs would live in the shadows, hunting and foraging for themselves, staying out of sight. These days, such dogs are rare, part domesticated, part wild. Frieda is such a dog.

In my time with Frieda, I have been struck again and again by her strength, hunting skills and instincts, loyalty, and ability to survive and adapt. It is possible that she could have survived a lifetime in the wilds of the Adirondacks. But I also know that she was savvy enough to move closer to civilization, where her options were greater, and the odds for her babies stronger. This was where she would engage in a long and remarkable cat-and-mouse game with the growing number of people who tried to catch her. This was a dog that knew how to take care of herself.

I could imagine that part of her life vividly.

The man opened the door of his truck, looked up and down the deserted highway, then got out and came around to open the door on the other side.

He said nothing to the dog; he simply reached in, tugged on her collar, and dragged her to the side of the road. He went back to the truck and pulled out a half-empty bag of kibble and took it a few feet into the woods, out of sight, and threw it on the ground.

Their relationship had always been detached, businesslike, but he was her human, and she was centered on him, obedient and loyal to him. He had fed her every day, and she had sought his approval and attention, even if she rarely got either.

"Hey," he said, "I want to give you a fighting chance. Bye, now." He stomped heavily, shooing her away from the highway, then turned to look at her, glanced up and down the road again, and climbed back into the truck, accelerated, and sped off. She stood for a long time watching the red taillights grow smaller on the big highway, listening to the sound of the engine she knew so well.

She was disoriented, confused, anxious. She lifted her nose and ears, and the stories of the woods revealed themselves to her, the smells, the sounds. She sensed everything deep in the ground, on the forest floor, the running, fighting, eating, dying. Buried in her genetic memory, a flood of messages and colors and smells and images were released by the sights and sounds around her. Her complex and deeply embedded instincts began to stir. She knew she had to find shelter. She knew she had to find food, for herself and for the creatures growing inside her, already changing her.

She kept listening to the highway sounds, looking for the man to come back, seeking out the particular sound of his truck amid the others she heard rumbling from either direction. It was a dark, cool night. She heard footsteps close and swiveled, and came nearly face-to-face with a doe, who, as startled as she, turned and vanished through the woods. The dog put her nose to the ground and recorded the smell.

She began to explore the forest. She found berries, pockets of moisture. She found the smell of a dead animal, and she rolled in it, over and over. She was moving deeper into the forest, but always listening for the man and for his truck.

After a few hours, she returned to the side of the highway, to look for the man and for the food he had left. She ate some of the kibble, but she was more thirsty than hungry. She'd been that way ever since the growth of her belly.

She smelled water, heard a creek beyond the thickness of the trees. It was getting dark, and cold. There were no cars on the road, no human sounds. No voices of people. No fence or woman carrying treats. No kind boy. No man bringing her food. No people coming by to bang on her fence, to try to get inside.

She lowered her tail, her ears, and her nose and moved quietly through the pine trees, around some brush, through a small meadow, closer to the stream.

At the stream, she drank, looked around, saw a woodchuck skittering, smelled a beaver's dam, heard the first hoot of an owl. Thou-

sands of bats began fluttering out of the trees, and gnats and mosquitoes began circling.

The wind rustled through the pines, and the dog knew she had to find shelter. She saw some rocks by the side of a hill and approached them, but there were strong smells coming from inside when she put her nose to an opening, and she withdrew.

Suddenly, she smelled something different, something new, right below her. She froze, barely breathing, not moving a muscle. She heard a rustling sound, looked down, saw a hole, and silently plunged her snout into it. It was a rabbit's nest, concealing a mother and some babies. She heard the squealing, the fright, the mother's frantic clawing and digging, trying to get out to lure the dog away, but it was too late. It was all over in a second.

The dog had burrowed with her nose, torn open the hole with her paws and claws, fed herself, fed her babies.

She had not considered this, thought about it, deliberated. She'd simply acted, as her instincts told her to do. She was in transition, not waiting for a human to feed her but already alert, awake to the knowledge that she had to feed herself.

She would not fight for space as she would for food. She fought and killed only when she needed to. She walked deeper into the woods, farther from the road, farther from her former life. Several miles in, she looked up a slope and saw giant boulders piled up, one on top of another, several trees fallen over them.

She heard steps and paused, and saw, for the first time, a shadowy black bear moving quietly along a deer path. She froze, growled softly, then checked herself. She raised her nose to take in the smell of this strange creature, then lowered her head to the ground until it was gone. A brown-and-black dog, she would be invisible on the forest floor when she was still, and she knew to do this. She had no experience in the forest, but her memory was strong and full of images of the past. Her instincts, her prey drive, were sharp and focused. She was already a different dog.

Creeping up the hill, she saw an opening in the big stones, and three fallen trees draped over it. The opening was not visible from the meadow below. You had to be right in front of it. She listened carefully and stuck her nose in. There was nothing in there, but she smelled feces of various kinds—mice, squirrels, perhaps.

The wind had come up, and it had begun to rain lightly. The temperature was dropping. Here was shelter—dark, small, protected.

Her days took on predictable patterns. Most predators in the forest ignored her; they were used to her now. Like the coyotes she heard yipping in the dark and the solitary foxes she saw trotting through the woods, she quickly discovered different kinds of food—berries, apples, nuts, wild grass, some wildflowers, skunks, chipmunks, rabbits, moles, mice, even the fresh carcasses of animals who had died or been hunted by hawks and owls or coyotes.

She began to evolve. She would find some heavy brush by the meadow and lie down, still, until a rabbit or turkey came by. She would stick her nose into nesting holes and surprise her prey. She was soon leaner, stronger, her coat heavier. She did not eat as regularly as before, but when she ate, she would gorge on a fat rabbit or hapless skunk, or a nest of chipmunks.

She retreated into her shelter when it was cold or raining and made sure to leave her scent and droppings there, to keep other animals out. She began to bring in twigs and bits of brush, to make a den for herself, and for her babies.

The weather got colder, and she spent more time inside, rest-

ing, staying warm. Every few days, she would explore, follow trails, listen for sounds. One day, she came to a house, deep in the woods, off by itself, and she watched as a man walked out with a bag and put it in a large can. She smelled the food—meat, too—all the way off in the brush, and the next morning, when the people drove off, she crept down, nosed open the can, and ate the food and bones they had left behind. She raised her head in the air and heard more sounds, smelled more things miles away, down to the south.

The winter came suddenly, and it was difficult. It was hard to move around; she was more conspicuous, and her prey was now buried deep in tunnels and nests, many of the small animals hibernating. She tried to hunt in the drifting snow, in the cold and ice, but her stomach was heavy, it was very cold. Her paws, unused to the ice and the cold, began to crack and bleed and were painful, and her joints grew stiff, slower. She grew weaker, thinner.

She found some bark, and some rotting berries. But it was not much nourishment for her. One day, she made her way back to the house where she had found the garbage. She came to understand that there was food around the few houses that dotted the landscape. Sometimes humans would see her and leave food for her. Other times she would forage for the many kinds of food humans threw away, left lying around, put in heaps outside in the ground.

She found a door left open in the shed behind the house, and there was a blanket and some kibble there. She began to spend her nights there. If a human approached, she would vanish, find another cave, another space beneath fallen trees, another shed.

She was uncertain about people. She had never really attached to any human other than the boy, and the wild and undomesticated part of her seemed to expand in the woods, become more dominant.

Moving would have become harder, as the babies grew larger. As the time got close, she simply stayed in her shed or cave.

Late one winter night, she gave birth to her pups in a wooden shed deep in the woods.

Her instincts took over now. She nursed the pups, cleaned them, growled them to sleep, or off her teats, or away from one another. The first few weeks, she barely got up, except to eat and to go outside to eliminate and urinate. She cleaned the babies, fed them from her swollen teats, leaned against them to give them warmth, tolerated their sharp teeth and growing appetites.

The pups began to move, to walk outside the shed, to look for food on their own. Somehow, she was separated from her pups. They ran off, or they died, or they were captured.

She looked for her babies, but their scents and sounds were gone, and she realized they were gone, too. Something—perhaps hunger, perhaps pursuit—made her move south. She began drawing closer to the things that might sustain her, coming across more homes, more people, more garbage, gardens, and barns.

She began moving out of the wild.

Just north of Glens Falls is SUNY Adirondack (formerly called Adirondack Community College), a nonresidential state university that draws farm kids and young people from the Adirondacks.

The college sits on a sprawling modern campus in Queensbury, on the southern edge of the Adirondack Park. It was perfect for Frieda. The brick buildings are spread out, with vast parking lots, the campus surrounded by woods and even some cornfields. The grounds offer many places for a dog to run and hide, to find food or shelter. It was a good place for a dog with the ability to move back and forth between civilization and the woods. It was also a good place for dog-loving students to leave offerings for the animal they had increasingly come to worry about and admire.

This is where we know Frieda ended up. This is where she drove her rescuers crazy, and figured out how to live, eat, and avoid capture for nearly a year. It was the perfect place for this dog, after her long journey through the forests. There were rabbits and mice and turkeys and skunks and chipmunks to find and eat, and garbage cans all around the numerous homes. People put food out behind their houses for her, and there were plenty of sheds, garages, woodpiles, and pallets to creep into at night.

There were trash cans all over the campus, where an enterprising dog could find food. Discarded sandwiches, pizza crusts, and other treats littered the grounds. There were giant dumpsters, filled with garbage waiting to be picked up. There was a cafeteria, emitting strong smells of food all day.

There were plenty of dangers, too. Trucks and cars on busy roads. Other dogs who challenged her and attacked her, farmers and other people with guns who shot at stray dogs, people afraid for their children who threw rocks at her, and the people in the black animal rescue vans, with their flashing lights, who seemed to follow her wherever she went.

People tried to coax her into their homes. To catch her. To tempt her. To trick her. Nobody could. She could sense a trap, smell food with chemicals, read the intentions of the men and women in the black trucks, who called to her, left food for her, carried snares and nets and set out big crates and traps. She could smell their intensity; she registered their focus on her, read their plans.

She knew how to hunt, and how not to be hunted.

There was a woman there who changed her life.

The young woman was named Gina. She noticed a dog prowling around at night and left food for her out in the woods, on the northern edge of the campus. She worked at an animal shelter, and she and her colleagues began to try to trap the dog they referred to as "ACC," for "Adirondack Community College," using food as bait.

Gina, now twenty-eight, works as a vet tech outside of Charleston, South Carolina. She left the Northeast in 2008 after her husband lost his job during the recession. The Queensbury SPCA, where Frieda was eventually taken, and where Gina worked, gave me her name and helped me locate her.

They still talk about Frieda at the shelter, officials there told me. As stories about her spread through the campus, students began to leave food for her behind the garbage cans at one of the administration buildings.

"You would rarely see her," recalled David, a shelter worker, now living in Saratoga and working as a vet tech while attending college. "Even the kids never saw her. This was a really unusual animal, a really remarkable animal, more like a wolf than a dog. She was fast and agile and smart and could take care of herself."

ACC was prone to chasing trucks, motorcycles, sometimes even bicycles. People were afraid for themselves and their dogs, even though she had never harmed anyone. Residents who lived around the college didn't want to see a big dog roaming the neighborhood, pawing through garbage, and potentially chasing after their kids. "She was a frightening dog, especially at night," Gina remembers. "People would see her running out of the woods, running in the moonlight, and they thought they were seeing a werewolf. She is not a mean dog, not at all, but you wouldn't know that to look at her. She would surprise people, appearing out of nowhere, and then vanishing into nowhere."

Gina's stories were very familiar to Maria and to me. It was eerie to see the way Frieda would hear or see something in the woods and simply melt into the trees as if she could make herself invisible. I could only imagine how she might scare the wits out of some suburban family near the college campus.

The shelter got a lot of calls about her, many of which were complaints.

Workers tried food laced with sedatives. They used other dogs as bait. They left steak and chicken in the woods, and set string traps, designed to catch her legs without harming them. They brought huge crates, put meat inside them, and left them in the woods and retreated out of sight. "The meat was always, always gone," said one of the shelter workers.

ACC assumed a legendary status on campus, as well as at the local animal shelter. If the students loved the renegade mystery dog, they almost all wanted to see her captured and, hopefully, adopted.

A number of different shelter workers—even some local state troopers and Warren County sheriff's deputies—tried to lure ACC into traps, bait her with meat, even trap her with nets and tranquilizer darts. Some local residents left food in their garages, tried to lure her into their homes.

"She was the savviest dog I ever went after," Gina said. "Most dogs are tired and frightened out in the woods or the streets. Most of them are hungry. You can almost always catch them with food. We never had so much trouble finding or capturing any dog as we did with ACC," she noted. "She seemed to know what we were doing, as if she had a spy inside the shelter. It was sort of a joke, asking each other who ACC's spy was. I'd tried leaving meat out for her, just to get her to trust me, to get her used to me. She would wait until I was far away, then rush up and grab it. Usually, she would ignore it. She never went near drugged food, came within range of a dart gun, or went near a trap."

Gina said she saw ACC only two or three times. When people called, she would drive the van out to the last sighting, but the dog would always be gone. Unlike most dogs, Gina thought, ACC was comfortable out in the woods that ringed the campus. She never got the feeling that ACC wanted to be caught, as most dogs did.

Toward the end of that winter, Gina remembers, a week-long torrential downpour flooded many of the streets around the college and turned the woods into a swampy bog. The workers at the shelter worried about ACC. They stepped up their efforts to trap her, and to try and get her adopted. The shelter had a new sedative drug that was guaranteed to be odor-free and undetectable, even to the nose of a hunting dog.

Shelter workers stopped to get some Big Macs and laced them with the new sedatives. Two hours later, they got a phone call that a dog matching ACC's description had been found staggering behind the school library and had collapsed there. They rushed over.

Gina was there for the capture. "She was sick, we think," she recalls. "The vet thought ACC had eaten something that made her sick, some rotten garbage or an infected animal. We found some worms in her stool, and she was not herself. We just put a collar on her with a pole we use, and she came along. She was done. There was no resistance, which is how I knew she was sick."

Gina was mesmerized to finally meet the dog she had been pursuing for so long. She thought ACC was beautiful, and the dog was not aggressive in any way to her or anyone else at the shelter. "It was as if she knew the game was up," Gina said. "She didn't bark or cause us any trouble. She made a lot of noise at the other dogs when she got comfortable, but I visited her every day. She was no trouble at all."

ACC's Adirondack adventure was over. So was her long and arduous journey into the wild. At the shelter, she was examined by a vet. His notes said she was healthy but undernourished. ACC had some arthritis, perhaps from the cold, needed to be wormed, and showed some signs of mild kidney trouble. She had numerous scrapes, scabs, and tick bites. Her teeth were cleaned, and she was scrubbed, brushed, and bathed.

Then they put her up for adoption.

ACC was in the SPCA of Upstate New York, in Queensbury, for nearly a year. During that time, hundreds of people visited the shelter. None of them chose to take her home.

Shelter workers remember her as quiet and well-behaved, wary but willing to be handled. Sometimes she barked at the other dogs, but mostly she just paced her kennel and studied the many people who came to the shelter looking for dogs and passed her by. She grew quiet, even lethargic. She was very well cared for, but life in a cage was a far cry from her freedom in the Adirondacks.

For many shelters, nine months is a long time to harbor an animal. ACC was getting short on time. She seemed unadoptable.

People would look at her, see the "rottweiler-shepherd" tag, and walk away. They were worried about their kids. Or other people's kids. Or the neighbors. Or the insurance. Or their other dogs.

Maria came to the shelter in the spring of 2003. She was not worried about any of those things. She took Frieda home to West Hebron the next day.

Frieda and I drove to Warrensburg later that spring. I pulled over near the freeway exit, got out of the car, and walked around to the other side. Frieda had a leash on her. When I opened the door, she willingly hopped out. We walked a few yards into the forest, and immediately, we were shrouded in darkness.

There was a deer path off to the left, and we followed it. Frieda's ears went back, and her head began to swivel back and forth, scanning the woods. She froze several times, subsequently diving with her nose into holes in the ground that were not visible to me. She had transformed herself instantly into a vigilant hunter, unaware of me, totally focused, ready to pounce. It seemed clear to me that she had been in this area before. She seemed confident, sure of what to do.

This experience—walking into the woods with her, imagining her life in the Adirondacks—was transformative, a powerful spiritual exercise that enabled me to understand her.

Few dogs in America get to make a lot of decisions about much of anything. Food is brought to them, they are walked on leashes, kept away from most public or work spaces. Their lives are completely bounded by often loving owners who consciously deprive them of every opportunity to make mistakes or decisions and learn from them. Our society and our legal system rigorously restrict the movement of dogs, and our litigious culture encourages their isolation.

Frieda had lived a completely different kind of life. In the auto body shop and out in the woods, she was on her own. She made decisions all day. She hunted and guarded, guarded and hunted.

I had to help her come to a different consciousness. One with another human in it, one where she learned basic commands and obedience, quieted her ferocious guarding and hunting instincts, and channeled them in a completely different direction.

I was beginning to understand her. She was not a "bad dog," or a troubled child, or a menace. Her powerful instincts for loyalty and protection were tools for me to use, to co-opt, not to challenge or punish. I needed to make them work for me, for us.

When we returned home, I told Maria about the day in the woods and about my new ideas. She just nodded and smiled.

Maria is not really into dog training, or the endless animal strategizing I engage in.

To me, life with animals is kind of like chess: they make a move; you make a move. Maria favors a more direct approach: open the gate and see what happens. She is an artist through and through. Her head is filled with colors and light and emotions, a kaleidoscope of love, energy, and imagination that never stops whirling and changing. I am different, and so are dogs. We focus on tasks. We use different instincts. We are, at least some of us, more cautious and wary.

Maria has neither an instinct nor a gift for redirecting or anticipating the behavior of animals. And, to be honest, she has little patience for either, seeing me as overly cautious, even neurotic on the subject. What she brings to the dogs is love and attention—unconditional, gentle, and consistent. And they love her for it. All of them, especially Frieda.

Maybe her way is right. But I have a different view. We get into trouble with animals when we don't think things through, when we don't understand enough about them or us. So I was ready to approach Frieda in a completely different way. To offer her a new idea of work. To test my own limits of patience—and of love. More than ever, I was coming to love Frieda. To admire this brave and resourceful creature who had come up against some of the worst things human beings have to offer and had kept her great heart.

Thousands of years ago, if the cave drawings are to be believed, dogs came together with humans and guarded their fires and caves, helped them find food, warned them away from wolves and other dangerous animals, fought and sacrificed for them, protected them from the many dangers of the night, and of the day.

Frieda was this kind of dog, and I had shifted from being wary of this out-of-control creature to being excited at the prospect of earning her trust, of showing her how to live safely in our world.

That night, when we got home from the forest, Frieda came over to me and lay down at my feet, the first time she had ever done that. I leaned over and tried to pat her head. She growled, took my arm in her mouth, and held it. She seemed to stop breathing, and so did I. Why, I wondered, was I so different from Sean? And then, of course, the answer hit me, as it should have much earlier. It was Maria. She was protecting Maria. She was, after all, the dog who kept men away.

Okay, not so fast, I thought. She's not giving it away.

"Thanks for not taking it off," I said, pulling my arm out slowly.

Chapter Fifteen

The Lesson of the Asian Pear

Two of the most important words I have ever learned are "drop it." Drop whining about the divorce. About money. About the way I was raised as a kid. About my family. About being lonely or sad, or crazy. It doesn't matter, really. We all have ups and downs in our lives, we are all afraid sometimes, or struggling, and if we are wise, we move on and just try to do better.

I think dogs know this intuitively. You will never hear a dog whine about the past, about being mistreated, about disappointment in humans. They live in the moment, accept their lives, and move forward. This is something they know, but I am just learning.

At this point, Maria and I were living in a world of panic, a sea of it. We panicked about health, money, the managing of our lives. We panicked about guilt—our divorces, family issues, a tangled web of unhealthy and unsupportive friendships.

We panicked about the recession, the price of things, whether or not we could get our work done, the farm. We panicked about Frieda.

I had heard about panic attacks for years—divorce also—but never thought either would have much to do with me or my life. These were things that happened to other people, people less together and fortunate than me.

The American Psychiatric Association says that panic attacks—periods of intense fear and apprehension—are among the most "intensely frightening, upsetting and uncomfortable experiences of a person's life and may take days to initially recover from."

Looking back, I realized I had been experiencing panic attacks for years. So had Maria, and we were both nearly crippled at times by their physical effects: exhaustion, headaches, sleeplessness, sweating, disorientation, rapid heartbeat, dizziness, nausea.

Maria would nearly go into shock, so exhausted she would sleep for hours, and I would be so terrified and drawn that I couldn't work. Different things set each of us off. There were so many triggers for me: bills, letters or emails from my divorce lawyer, telephone calls, invitations to family functions, awful stories on the news, book deadlines, contact with some members of my family.

We were porous, the fear inside us locked in this synergistic energy exchange with the outside world. We could not bear to hear the news. Avid readers, we could not read. Long-time movie lovers, we couldn't get through a single movie or watch TV. In previous summers, I had always loved watching baseball, but that year, I couldn't make it through a single game. My daughter, a baseball writer in New York City, was baffled. I couldn't explain it to her.

We learned to spot the symptoms in each other quickly, and we had a set of drills, mantras, exercises for each other. Maria would take my hand, wipe my forehead with a damp cloth, rub my feet. It's not real, we would tell each other. It feels real, but it is not real. "Do you know it's not real?" she would ask.

I would do the same. "Something is wrong with me," Maria would say weakly, so softly I could barely hear her. And I would bring her tea, play quiet music, get her to smile.

Time and again, over and over, we brought each other back to life. Back to reality. Back to the world. We couldn't prevent these attacks, and we couldn't make them disappear, but they became less intense, less frequent. We learned to tell ourselves these stories, these mantras. We grew familiar with the signs that meant that one of us was beginning to slip into a panic attack and could sometimes head the whole experience off.

My feeling about panic attacks evolved once I began talking to therapists about them and doing some research of my own. They are mysterious. There might be a biochemical cause for some people, post-traumatic stress for others. There is surely a physical component to them, as the body reacts to so much stress in many different ways.

The clearest explanation was this: Maria and I, both traumatized in youth, learned to live with fear and coped with it in many different ways—mostly by finding ways to suppress or transfer it. Later in life, suddenly out of long marriages, out in the open, alone and seemingly unprotected, we were simply terrified. We had not learned how to live in the world. And now we had to.

After a while, some of the panic attacks became a joke. We'd get up in the morning, and Maria would whisper, "I don't have enough time," and I'd whisper back, "I don't have enough money." And we learned to laugh.

We made some friends. We found some restaurants. We read books, visited each other, called each other on our cellphones. We did our work, shared our insights, forgave our setbacks and defeats. What a beautiful thing this was, two people patching their busted-up lives together, our dogs silent witnesses and companions.

Bit by bit, we returned to life. Saw people from our old lives, eased back into the world, to our work. It was a creative existence, for sure. All day, Maria stitched together her quilts and her pot holders, put them on her website, learned about packaging and shipping, postage and taxes.

I began to write again, holed up in my corner study, calling Maria when I felt the panic surging, or taking the calls when she felt it. We got through it. We took naps, walked every day on the path, snow or sun, cold or warm. We hiked up the hill. We drove to Glens Falls and walked those gritty streets. We went to inns and galleries in Vermont. We snuck off to New York City, to Brooklyn, to visit my daughter, go to museums, find dim sum in Chinatown.

And then, as the therapists had predicted, the panic began to ease. I started to manage my money and found a financial adviser who understood the lives of creative people and crazy people—often the same thing. I began to recover physically, emotionally, spiritually.

Maria and I never quit on each other, never got sick of each other, never let go of each other. Each of those daily routines and small kindnesses was a step toward healing, toward life.

Oddly enough, technology helped save both of us. Maria created her own blog, fullmoonfiberart.com, and she began posting photos of her quilts and pot holders. I wrote about my depression and fear on my blog, and I realized, as many people in trouble do, that I was not alone. Magical helpers appeared, and reappeared, popped up behind signposts and trees, sent me messages from all over the world. My readers encouraged me, cheered me, supported me.

The dogs anchored me: Walks in the woods. Cuddles with Lenore. My therapist challenged me to understand that I had lost perspective and was not seeing the world clearly. She told me that I could manage my life and that she supported my relationship with Maria.

I stopped seeing my psychoanalyst. I stopped taking sleeping pills and medicine to soothe my nerves. I stopped seeing doctors at all. I didn't want to live a life of tests, pills, and worry. I would take my chances. I wanted every day of the rest of my life to be as good and filled with love and light as they could possibly be. For me, Maria was the light. When I look at her, I smile. She knows what I am thinking before I think it. She tells me to shut up when I need to be quiet, and laughs at me when I am being foolish. She supports every good thing I do, genuinely seems to think that I am handsome, and I devote every day of my life to making her feel happy and supported.

One day, after Maria became my "girlfriend"—I loved having a "girlfriend" again—I was shopping in my local market. Walking through the produce section, I picked up an Asian pear on an impulse. I don't usually buy such exotic fruits, and in a small town people speak their minds and there are no secrets of any kind. When I was checking out, the cashier—her badge said Anne Marie—turned to me and asked, "Why are you buying an Asian pear? They're expensive!" I said I was buying it as a surprise for my girlfriend.

Anne Marie's whole tone and demeanor changed. "Why, that's sweet. It's a good thing to do," she said approvingly, even though she clearly thought the pears were not a sensible purchase and might even have been a rip-off. "It's the little things."

This prompted a minor explosion of comment and approval from the women in line behind me, and the ones in the line next to me. "My husband would never do that," said the woman directly behind me, unloading her groceries onto the moving ramp. "And she's right," she said. "Remember this. It's the little things. I don't care if I ever have a diamond. But if he would bring me flowers once in a while, that would mean the world to me. That he thought about me."

A woman in the next line came over to tell me that men forget to show love in this way, and it's hurtful. "Keeping doing it," she said, "and your girlfriend will love you forever." I was surrounded by five or six women clapping me on the back, praising me, all just for buying an Asian pear.

This incident made a deep impression on me. I saw in these women's faces, and heard in their words, a lot of love and a lot of hurt and a lot of sadness, and I have, as I promised, never forgotten it. How little it would have taken to make them happy, and how little they wanted. Never become that small, I told myself, that I don't regularly celebrate the amazing woman in my life.

That day I made a list of things I must always do to make Maria happy and show her how much I love her. While I am far from being a perfect partner, I have honored this list and have kept my promise to myself and to the women at the supermarket that day. When Maria and I eventually married, I went back to the market and found the cashier and gave her flowers to thank her. She burst into tears.

"I can't believe you did this," she said.

"It's the little things," I said.

This is my list:

1. Every day I will tell Maria how much I love and appreciate her, and never assume that she knows it.

2. Every time I shop for groceries, I will bring her an Asian pear. Or the goat cheese she loves. Or the salmon she likes.

Or something new that she might enjoy, as a surprise. (It costs very little, and I love to see the look of delight on her face as she helps unpack the bags and looks for it.)

3. Every day, I will tell her how much I admire her work, how good it is, how much people will like it. (She tends to dismiss this as the encouragement of someone biased in her favor. But she also smiles, drinks it up. It is fuel for her, and people need fuel for their lives, for their dreams.)

4. Every day I will cook at least one meal for her. (She can cook, and does, but when you cook for someone, you are thinking of them, nurturing them, nourishing them.)

5. When she's sick or can't sleep, I'll tell her stories, sing her songs, rub her stomach, cast a spell on her. Love heals. It really does. I'm living proof of it.

6. If I am angry, I will say so. If I am irritated, I will tell her. I'll be honest with her always.

7. Every week, I will get her a gift. A small thing. A second-hand leather jacket from a thrift shop. A bracelet. An old pin from an antiques dealer's junk box. Note cards. A porcelain figure to put in her studio barn. (I found a vintage clothes dealer online and stored her sizes, so when there is a dress or scarf or funky pair of sandals I think she will like, I can just click on it. She scolds me and tells me not to buy her things, but she lights up like a Christmas tree every time I give one to her.)

8. I will be open to new things. To talking to animals. To wearing something other than blue. To going tubing on the beautiful Battenkill River. To accepting Maria's compliments.

9. I will find new things for us to share. An old inn in Vermont, Thai food, meditation workshops, museums. While we are both very independent, the things we share form a center that holds us together, always.

10. I will listen. I am a talker more than a listener, but I am learning to listen. I want to learn to hear. I want Maria to always know that I will hear what she tells me and will consider it carefully, even if I don't like it, which is often the case. (If you learn to listen, you'll find the great lessons of life in unexpected places.)

Looking back, I think Maria and I had spent much of our lives trying and failing to communicate with the people around us, for reasons that were our fault as much as anybody's. We always felt out of sync with the world, on the outside, peering in. She was an artist who could never seem to break into the inner circle of the art world, and I was a writer as removed from the literary life as one could get. We were refugees, pilgrims, wanderers, having finally drifted to a tiny town in upstate New York, a perfect hideout. And there, of all places, we found each other.

If she taught me selfless love, I taught her how to communicate with the outside world, something she had not yet been willing or able to do. And to use some of the new tools of the digital age to make and market her work. To stay in touch with friends. To buy the things she needed to make her quilts, streaming pieces, and pot holders. When I met her, she was a Luddite, disdainful of computing and clearly terrified of it.

I love technology, and Apple devices litter the farmhouse, including an iPhone. Upstate, cell towers are few and far between, and the interrupted call is standard.

This became a metaphor for our ability to communicate despite great obstacles. We managed to connect with each other in incomplete thoughts, unfinished sentences, dropped calls. After we had been together a few months, we knew precisely when our calls would be cut off, at which tree, by which farm, near which cows. We became expert at starting a sentence in one town and finishing it in another, or when somebody was pulling into the driveway. We had that quality people in love have of feeling that nothing had really happened until we had shared it. We still have that feeling.

Through all of these interrupted and unfinished messages, we understood each other perfectly, and communicated all the time. "Hey," Maria would say as she left work, "I'm on the way home—" I would put the phone down and wait five minutes, and when she got to McEachron Hill Road in Argyle (I always knew where she was from where the calls stopped and started) she would finish the sentence: "—and I had a great morning, except Virginia slugged me with her shoe."

And then, when she got home, we'd go over it all again, and I'd fill her in on the two or three things I had accomplished and felt and worried about since she had left.

Sometimes people in relationships like to tell their schedules to each other: *I'm going here, I'm going there.* Maria and I shared feelings. I felt bad, felt scared, felt better. And more and more, it was better.

I told Maria from the first that I did not want unconditional love. I wanted a relationship that worked, that was conditional upon affection, respect, and support. If it stopped working, I said, save yourself, walk away, find love somewhere else.

And in that odd way, our love became unconditional. Because it was free and good and because we worked at it and wanted it so much. Our panic attacks began to decrease. It turned out we could take care of ourselves. We could make decisions.

And the best decision either of us made was to love the other, to take the other by the hand and walk into life. Whatever happens, it is a decision I will never regret making. Neither, I believe, will she.

Every day I had been asking Maria to marry me. It was getting to be kind of fun, a ritual, although I was deadly serious. At first she said no. Then she said, "Thanks, maybe one day." Then one day, finally, she said yes.

And I knew then that everything would be all right.

We set a date: June 12, 2010. The only day I can remember as being comparable in terms of happiness to the day Maria agreed to marry me was November 5, 1981, when my daughter, Emma, was born.

I was certain now that Maria and I would be living together, so it became even more important that Frieda get settled. The trips to South Glens Falls and the Adirondacks had given me some new ideas about Frieda's world, and the ways in which I might connect with her.

However, the very sight of my dogs still sent Frieda into a frenzy of barking, growling, and lunging. She went out of control when she even glimpsed Izzy, Lenore, or Rose in the yard.

One day, in the studio barn, I had Maria put a leash on Frieda, and I walked her toward the yard, where my dogs sat quietly, watching. Frieda made them nervous. They didn't really know how to react to her, except for Rose, who stiffened and growled and seemed determined to challenge her. Even as Rose began lunging, I walked Frieda across the road, right to the edge of the gate. She began barking and leaping and jumped up, as if to go over the fence. Without thinking, really, I shot my foot out to block her and caught her in the belly. I could not let her jump over the fence. I had planned to get her to lie down and then reward her but had accidentally kicked her instead.

Frieda yelped and dropped to the ground in a perfect lie-down. She growled and whined a bit but stayed almost completely still, and she was no longer even looking at the dogs or trying to get over the fence.

Of course, I thought, Stella's husband must have trained her by using his foot. That kind of training is unimaginable to me, but it was now clear that Frieda had been waiting for the command to be quiet, for the right command to be given. Somehow, I seemed to have given it. I reached into my pocket and tossed some beef jerky to her, and she ate it quickly and hungrily, more readily than usual.

Having smelled the jerky, Rose, Izzy, and Lenore came over to the fence. I tossed them some, too.

In my experience, there is nothing that calms a dog more

than lying down and eating something, as long as no other dogs or people are too close to the food. And a great way to get dogs comfortable with one another is to have them eat their food at the same time, a safe distance apart from one another.

Frieda desperately needed calming training, but I was always struggling to get her attention. Though I had not attempted to kick her, just to stop her, I could guess that she had been kicked in her life, and it was clearly something she paid attention to. My gesture couldn't have hurt much, but it had surprised her. And, suddenly, I had her full attention. I tossed some more treats around, then told her to get up, and I walked her along the fence as the other dogs bounded around on the other side.

I was excited. I could see that Frieda liked having Lenore walk alongside her. When I told Lenore, "Sit," Frieda watched as the Lab sat. I did this three times, and on the fourth attempt, Frieda sat down alongside Lenore. Lenore kept nuzzling her, and I was surprised to see Frieda's tail wag. I went back and got Izzy, who has no interest in other dogs or in fighting, and he simply walked ahead of us, onto the path. Frieda growled and lunged toward him at first, but after a few minutes, she and Izzy were sniffing the grass.

This interaction was not all that dramatic, but it definitely represented a turning point. I could get Frieda to lie down now. I could begin training her near my dogs, so that she would calm down long enough to get to know them, and to accept them as part of her world. To see them as animals to protect and socialize with rather than creatures to attack and drive away from Maria.

"Maybe one day . . ." I said, but Maria, reading my mind,

shook her head. She knew I meant that maybe one day Frieda would be able to come into the house. She didn't dare imagine it.

I've written a bunch of books about dogs, and trained a lot of them, and one of the things I have learned is to not get cocky, a natural trait in impatient and distractible souls like me.

Frieda was soon to remind me of that.

But even so, something had changed. Frieda looked at me with new respect since I'd accidentally kicked her. And the truth was, I was coming to love her indomitable spirit. She had been through enough to sink a dozen dogs, and had handled all of it, and was still trying to run my farm.

Chapter Sixteen

Dancing Naked in the Snow

One crisp, dark winter morning, I got up early to make breakfast for Maria. It was five A.M., and I had just let the dogs out. Frieda was still confined to her minimum-security facility in the backyard, a fenced-in area originally built for goats. I let her out of her crate first, as I usually did; later Maria would bring her back to the studio barn. The fence was just behind the farmhouse, and Frieda never gave me any trouble about going in there—she had been in her crate all night and seemed eager to go relieve herself and sniff around.

As I was making some oatmeal, I heard a strange shriek and thump in the backyard. I rushed out back and was, for once, speechless.

Frieda was just inside the gate of her compound, and she was sitting on a large animal, the sun coming up behind her. It was a deer, struggling and a bit in shock but very much alive. The deer were always hopping in and out of the fenced pastures, but they scattered at the sight of a dog. This one had not encountered a dog like Frieda before. Frieda wasn't biting or harming it. She was just sitting on it. She had clearly run it down and she was now treating it like a trophy, almost grinning with pride.

I was speechless. Dogs chase after deer all the time upstate, but they rarely, if ever, catch up with one, let alone run it down and sit on it.

"Frieda, get off that deer!" I sputtered. And she did. She hopped off and looked at me, a little abashed, while the deer scrambled to her feet and took off.

Two things about this incident struck me:

1. Frieda was one strong dog with a lot of prey drive. A lot.

2. Frieda listened to me when I told her to get off the deer.

My neighbors were never as impressed with me as when they heard that story. "She got a deer?" one man said incredulously. "That's quite a dog."

Yessir, I thought. That's my girl.

If there is one thing most of the dog lovers I know do not want to think of their beloved furry soul mates as having, it is a lot of prey drive. It is, I think, one of the reasons it's so important not to emotionalize our dogs too much. It is just too easy to misunderstand them.

Frieda is the living embodiment of this. Dogs are not like us, even though they love us and we love them. They come from a very different place than we do, and their genes carry a lot of very different impulses.

Dogs are all predators, descended from wolves. Breeding and domestication have altered that behavior in many dogs, but still, a lot of our beloved pets are quasi wolves, ready to stalk their prey, pounce, and chew them up.

Frieda had a powerful and strongly reinforced prey drive. Not only had she run off intruders at her fence in Glens Falls, but she'd had to run down food in the Adirondacks.

So this trait had been reinforced and intensified in her, for almost all of her life. She had not been trained in any conventional way, or taught any alternative or diversionary behaviors. She was all prey drive.

It was critical for me to understand this about her. All predators have a prey drive, and in the most natural and elemental state, that prey drive follows a specific sequence: the search, the eye-stalk, the chase, the grab bite, and, finally, the kill bite. In dogs of certain breeds, these steps have been either amplified or reduced by human-controlled and selective breeding.

The eye-stalk, for example, was familiar to me from watching Rose and Izzy herd sheep, or simply play and run on the path. Border collie breeders have used selective breeding to diminish the grab bite and the kill bite. But other impulses have been sharpened.

Shepherds do not want their dogs eating sheep, so border

collies stalk and chase and, occasionally, nip. Humans watching border collies work see them as being remarkably intelligent and intuitive, and they are, but it is their prey drive that gets them to focus so intensely on the work and to control much larger and less intelligent sheep. You will rarely hear people talk about prey drive on TV herding-trial shows or in rhapsodical herding books. And yet, I saw it all the time in Rose. Border collies are genetically the closest match to wolves in the canine spectrum. When you watch a border collie crouch down low and stalk the sheep, you see it clearly.

People also often mistake prey drive for play. When a golden retriever or Lab is chasing after a ball and romping through the grass with it, people beam, seeing their dogs as happy and fulfilled. They are also witnessing the development— the sometimes very healthy rechanneling—of the prey drive, the hunting and chasing instinct that almost all working dogs have, and many others as well.

The prey drive often shapes the most pronounced characteristics of a dog. Focused, it can lead to some amazing things— like herding sheep, sniffing out bombs, retrieving ducks. Unmanaged, it can cause serious trouble, from hyperarousal to fighting and other aggressive behaviors.

I've learned to be very cautious about play, or any behaviors that incite the prey drive, as these can bring out the very impulses in a dog I like to de-emphasize: arousal, hunting, mouthing, excessive chewing and licking, distraction. A dog who chases a ball all day is likely to be very excited, difficult to train, and a pest, sometimes even aggressive.

For this reason, I never permit playing of any kind in the house. It's easy to turn a dog on, not so easy to turn one off. So we play in the yard, in the meadows, on the paths. Not in the house.

It's important to socialize a dog, but I believe that few of them need to play much when they are older. Organized play for adults dogs is a very new and very American idea. Sometimes we make our dogs crazy, then blame them for it. I work hard to show my dogs how to do nothing. They all know how to be crazy. Dogs like Frieda—rottweilers and shepherds—get a lot of bad publicity and suffer for this, languishing in shelters or avoided altogether.

I felt I had broken through some of the crazy, wild impulses and instincts that raged inside Frieda's head. But if you live with dogs, and work with them, you know it is never quite that simple.

Frieda was beginning to understand, I think, that I was not going away, that Maria did not need protection from me, that I was not something to be wary of or driven off. Put differently, she was getting used to me, seeing me as part of the landscape rather than a danger to it. And that was a big step.

But I wasn't quite prepared for the depth of her drive, or the work I would have to put in to control it.

When I thought about it, and watched Frieda, her behavior made sense. She'd been placed in the worst possible position for her when she'd appeared in one of my barns. She'd been dropped, without much training or preparation, into the middle of a farm loaded with prey—chickens, cats, donkeys, and sheep.

And she went after all of them.

The most terrifying encounter was with the donkeys, who one day got through an open gate and into Frieda's confinement pen. I then put her in there without seeing them. Of all the prey behaviors, I noticed that the strongest in Frieda was the "chase" element. If something moved away from her, this seemed to trigger the most powerful response, which is probably what happened with the deer. I noticed that her bite reflexes were not as well developed (except when it came to chipmunks or rabbits). She had big teeth but not a strong bite behavior. It was running things down that got her going.

This happened with the two donkeys, who, seeing Frieda, began to back off and run away. She gave chase, and when Frieda is in chase mode, she is almost in a trance. It is nearly impossible to get her attention, or to get her to stop. I rushed from one end of the pen to the other, trying to avoid the donkeys and get in front of Frieda, although I wasn't sure what I would do if I caught her.

The donkeys were beginning to kick and snort, their eyes wide with panic, and Frieda was running hard, tongue to the ground, head low. There was a large ball in the yard that Lenore used to play with, and I grabbed it, knelt down, and threw it at Frieda's head as hard as I could, as close as I could get.

As with the accidental kick, it startled her, and she paused, looking to see where it had come from. She slowed just enough so that I could get in front of her, and I drew myself up, threw my arms out (trainers call this "doing the bear"), and simply said, "Stop." She did.

Her tongue seemed to be hanging down about a foot, and she was heaving and gasping for breath. So were the donkeys. I told Frieda to stay, and once again, she did. I was able to get to the rear gate and opened it wide enough that the donkeys rushed out. I have no doubt that one of these animals would have been badly hurt or killed if I had not gotten Frieda to stop that day.

The next week, Frieda slipped out the back door and went after a dog being walked up our road. Teddy was a small, loud poodle who came past the farm twice a day, which triggered every bit of protective instinct and prey drive in Frieda. She got a good running start on the long, tall fence and leapt right over it, landing in front of the astonished dog and his owner, a neighbor who lived down the road. Monica didn't rattle; she scooped the barking Teddy up in her arms just as I got to the street and yelled at Frieda to lie down, which she did. It was frightening to see Frieda barking, lunging, and foaming at this little dog, but once again I noted that she didn't bite or lunge, just made a lot of dreadful and frightening noise. And she did respond to my shouted command.

This also happened with the barn cats, who sometimes saw Frieda in the pen outside and ran up a tree or down the driveway. Of course, when they ran, Frieda would go into her trance and pursue them. When she saw the sheep, too, she would sometimes go into her stare and begin whining. So we were especially vigilant.

We always made sure there were no animals around when Frieda went out. I still couldn't get her to let me put a leash on her, but she did allow me to walk her, so I'd have Maria clip a leash or rope on her; then I would take her outside, put her in a lie-down while I fed the cats or the chickens, and walk her up into the pasture and have her lie down around the sheep. Every animal on the farm took off at the sight of Frieda—prey animals are great readers of dog intent—but this process worked, over time. It took six months before Frieda stopped lunging toward the cats or giving the donkeys that look.

Some animals in the forest didn't fare as well. Several times during our walks, when we were careless or distracted, Frieda would spot some animal out in the woods, slip her lead, and then suddenly and silently vanish.

Maria and I would be shocked; we searched, but we never saw or heard a sound from her. We walked into the woods, calling for her. We got the ATV and tried to flush her out, but we never could. The woods beyond the farm are deep and dark, and it was disturbing, to say the least, to think of Frieda running around out there. We worried that she would get lost, surrounded by coyotes, trapped by barbed wire, caught in deep brush.

The first few times this happened, we spent hours looking for her. But we quickly realized the futility of our efforts—we never managed to find her. Usually she'd be gone for three to five hours, and we learned to leave a gate or the barn door open and to put out food and fresh water for her. Eventually, she would appear, as quietly as she had gone. We never saw or heard her coming. Often, she would be covered in blood, her paws torn, her claws broken and bleeding. She would almost be in a trance, her tongue hanging down, and she didn't seem to hear us. She had been transported into a completely different space. She would gulp down a gallon of water, then sleep for hours, through the night and into the next morning. All we could do was get better leashes and collars and watch her more carefully. But once in a while, she would still slip away.

Nevertheless, when the wildness came out in her, it was an

amazing thing to see, a great affirmation of prey drive, a return to the wild.

I learned from each episode and began to develop a coherent, consistent theory of training her, aimed at reducing this intense drive.

Mostly I used alternative behavior theories. When we were near animals, I would offer her treats—biscuits, beef jerky, as well as verbal praise—rewarding her when she was looking away from the animals, or at me, or at the food. Although she wouldn't let me touch her, she seemed to appreciate the positive reinforcement. Her tail would wag slightly, and she'd seem at ease.

Slowly, this alternative way of looking at the world began to take hold, and we saw some small behavioral changes. Although she treed the barn cats several times, she seemed to realize that they were part of her world, not intruders. Since she no longer got to run or hunt, I saw her prey drive weaken. Reinforced to be still and calm, she began to calm down, to focus more on me and Maria, or on the other dogs.

I am an impatient person, and we live in an impatient, quick-fix world. I was frustrated by what I considered the slow progress Frieda was making, yet there was definitely progress. All I had to do was keep at it, keep working, stay positive, not push it too far or too fast—my great weakness as a dog trainer. And, to be honest, the dogs I already had didn't require all that much long-term patience. Lenore, Izzy, and Rose never ran off; they all stayed off the street, watched me closely, and followed directions. The thought of them taking off into the woods for five hours was almost unthinkable. And for dogs raised in a household like mine, why would they? They never had to use much prey drive, except for Rose in her herding work, and there was always a good supply of food and treats, attention and affection. My dogs always wanted to be with me, and now they always wanted to be with Maria, too. Frieda had a different upbringing, different traditions.

But still, small steps. I believe that at this point, Frieda had come to see that she was not the one responsible for running the farm. I was careful to be clear and positive but strong with her. I thought she was letting go of some of her dominance, almost happy to give up some of her presumed responsibility.

She could stop using her prey drive as her primary means of work and survival. I was working with her constantly. For the first time, I noticed her staring out the window of the studio barn in a relaxed way—not rigidly, in her guard stance, but more like an early retiree just taking in the view.

I always praised this, reinforced it with good words and food, and I encouraged Maria to do the same thing. When Frieda roared at the mailman or a truck, Maria learned to wait until she was quiet, and then reward her. Or reward her and distract her before she went off. More and more, this was working.

The prey drive is a series of instincts, not a conscious, moral, or reasoned decision, so Frieda would still react more quickly than she might actually think something through. For instance, if a chicken or cat ran past her or away from her, it would trigger the stalk-and-run behavior. It would happen in a flash, a microsecond. Fortunately, we hadn't gotten to test the grab-bite response yet, or the kill bite. My goal was not to get to that point. I imagine Frieda could have easily killed the chickens when she was chasing them, but she ended up instead with a mouthful of tail feathers. Was she going for the kill? I didn't know.

If Frieda was outside her fence and the donkeys were grazing up the hill, she would sit calmly. But if they started, or moved quickly, or ran for any reason, the wolf in her would come right out and she would take off after them.

Donkeys, sheep, and chickens are all prey to foxes, coyotes, and, in the past, wolves, so they are all very sensitive to a dog like Frieda zeroing in on them. They will ignore my other dogs—Lenore, for instance—but they are always aware of Frieda's presence, and they monitor her movements, even when she is far away. The sheep are among the world's best readers of prey drive, and you can see the prey drive in a dog just by watching them.

When we let Frieda out into her pen, the donkeys would form a protective half circle in front of the sheep, every time, something they never do with Lenore or the border collies. Prey animals are the best measure of predatory behavior there is. My chickens would always go on pecking right alongside the other dogs, but when Frieda came out of the house, they would immediately run for the barn.

One afternoon, Frieda had her rope on her, and I went to the studio barn and took her outside, picking up the rope and walking her to the edge of the pasture. The donkeys were standing by the water trough down at the bottom of the pasture gate. Frieda's ruff stood up, her head went down, and her ears flattened, and I heard the low rumble of her growl. I stuck my foot on the rope and pushed it to the ground. "Hey," I said, stepping around in front of her.

"Stay down."

In their natural environment, donkeys are prey, especially to wolves and big cats. Lulu and Fanny were wary and alert, and when I yelled for Frieda to go down, they both took off up the hill.

Frieda was off in a flash, out of my grasp, her prey-pursuit drive in full gear. She raced back and forth quickly, then went over the four-foot pasture fence, almost before I could move. Not only was my worst nightmare happening, but I had brought it about by being foolhardy, by expecting too much of her too soon, putting her in a situation that was dangerous for her and other animals.

Suddenly, she stopped and yelped. The long rope had caught on the fence post, and she was hanging off the gate, beginning to choke. I ran. Fortunately, I had my knife in my pocket, and I sawed through the rope in seconds.

I was furious. "No," I yelled, cuffing Frieda lightly along the side of the head. I try to be uniformly positive in my training, and I never hit my dogs; nor do I believe in that as a training method. But I have a temper, and Frieda had frightened me, taken me to the edge. I just lost it when I thought of what might have happened.

I am also human, and quite flawed, and I had succumbed to the human failing of attributing a person's motives to a dog. Here I had worked so hard, walked her so many times, tried to understand her, brought her into the life of the farm, tried to make a place for her with us. And this was how she rewarded me? Where was her sense of loyalty?

Of course I know that Frieda is not a bad dog and was not acting out of any evil or ungrateful motive. I had just figured out how big a role prey drive was playing in her life, and yet I'd put her in a position, without redirecting her, where she'd had almost no choice but to act on it. I was the one who should have been cuffed, not the dog.

I apologized to her, and she trotted along very willingly, not even looking at the donkeys. I hadn't anticipated Lulu and Fanny running, and that is what had triggered Frieda's lunge. And I'd been foolish for dropping the rope. (I'd wanted to get in front of her to give her some hand signals.) Okay, I said, live and learn. Move on. Don't be too rough on her. Don't be too rough on yourself. Pick it up again tomorrow.

I knew Maria had mostly given up on the idea of Frieda ever being in the farmhouse. She hoped Frieda would one day be able to hang out in the yard with the other dogs, but she thought that would be years away. And she just couldn't ever see Frieda in the farmhouse. Too many people and dogs, coming and going, all of which still upset Frieda greatly.

Besides, Maria had other problems to deal with. Although she had agreed to marry me, she was still worried that she would have no work or identity of her own. That she would become Mrs. Bedlam Farm. Mrs. Jon Katz. I saw the danger in that. If she came to feel that way, our relationship could be damaged, even disintegrate.

And that was, in many ways, the toughest issue for me, because it wasn't one I could argue convincingly. I was a biased and interested party. But by then, I don't think either one of us really had a choice. We had been fighting to be together for a long time. Not being together just seemed unimaginable, like failing Frieda.

Ours was a creative connection; that was the core of our relationship. We both advanced the idea of creative change. In difficult times, creative people get creative. They adapt.

Maria sold some quilts. She designed her low-priced pot holders to fit the struggling economy. If people couldn't afford her $300 quilts, then she would make small quilts—pot holders—and sell them for $15. It was a creative and agile idea, and it worked. That first Christmas, she sold three hundred of them, all over the world. She made pillows, iPad bags, cellphone bags, and smaller quilts with drawings, sketches, and free-motion sewing-machine images.

Sales weren't huge, but they were growing all the time. The business paid for itself and allowed Maria to be independent of me. This gave her confidence, showed her that people liked her work and would pay for it.

This was an old issue for her, only partially to do with her art. But it was very painful, and it had shut her down for a long time. I wanted to be as supportive as I could be, as supportive as she was of me.

But it was hard. Like Frieda, Maria had a worldview firmly implanted in her consciousness, and it would take a lot of work and time to change. I didn't know how much time either of us had to sort this out.

Maria was, at that point, especially fragile. Some mornings, she was frightened to even go into her studio to work. Succeeding was almost unimaginable to her. She had taken on a lot, was exhausted, worried. Through all of that struggle, all of that darkness, Maria had what I called her Achilles' heel—her sense of humor, the place I could always reach her. We had the same strange way of looking at the world and were quick to laugh and see irony and absurdity, and when she smiled, it was the most radiant and uplifting thing I ever beheld.

More than anything, I wanted to see that smile. Whenever I could, I tried to draw it out. It stretched from one end of her face to the other, and it pulled her up, almost every time. But that smile was hard to come by sometimes.

One night, she just crashed. She burst into tears and said she couldn't do it, couldn't make any more art. "Nobody will like it, nobody will buy it," she worried. She went to soak in a long, hot bath, something she always did when she was feeling especially low.

She had to go out and find a regular job, she said. She knew the economy was rough, and all of the artists she talked to spoke of little but their trouble selling anything. She stayed up all night crying, sitting by herself down in the living room, staring out at the road. She went over to the barn where Frieda was sleeping and sat with her for hours. She was simply beyond my reach, falling into a dark and remote place. Nothing I said made much of a difference.

We were both up all night. In the morning, Maria didn't feel like eating. She went across the road and took Frieda out, and then came in and kissed me goodbye and headed for her car. I had never seen her look so bleak and defeated. It was as if she had just run out of gas, lost the will to keep fighting this old battle with depression and fear.

It was pitch-black outside, and an icy winter wind was

howling around the farmhouse, blowing drifting snow around the pasture. I waited until Maria got into her car and the lights came on.

I should pause here and say that I am an extremely uptight and closed-up person when it comes to my body. I almost never permitted photos of me on my website or anywhere else. I never took my socks off, and even in the hottest weather I wore a hat, a heavy blue denim shirt, and jeans. I guess I had what they call a poor self-image, but I'd never cared for the way I looked, at any point in my life. Of all of the things that surprised me in those years, nothing was more shocking or confounding than Maria's insistence that I was handsome.

"You're crazy," I would say. I never believed the compliment, not for a second. I thought Maria's vision was just fuzzy, and that one day she would wake up to the reality of this horrifying man and scream and run off.

But that morning, I took off my bathrobe and nightshirt and grabbed my blue battery-charged wizard hat. Naked except for my slippers and the hat, I turned on the floodlights at the rear of the house, rushed out the back door, plowed through the snow and ice, and started to sway back and forth in the headlights of Maria's car.

I began to sing and dance, the lights on my hat flashing red and blue.

I don't remember what I sang, but I do remember jumping up and down, like a medicine man at a ceremony in some cheesy old movie.

Maria was looking over her shoulder, about to back up, when she noticed the floodlight and then me, dancing back and forth in front of the car. I could see her jaw drop, and this million-dollar delighted smile broke out, brighter than all the other lights.

She laughed, shook her head, and started applauding me. Then she got out of the car, came over to me, and gave me a big hug.

I danced for as long as I could stand it, and I could not stand it for long. Then I rushed back into the house. The dogs were gathered by the kitchen door, Rose staring at me incredulously, with her most pronounced "he's lost his mind again" look.

In a couple of minutes, my cellphone rang.

"That was the most beautiful dance I ever saw," Maria said. She was still laughing.

After that, whenever she got too down, I would dance naked in the snow.

Unfortunately, it was a cold, tough winter. But my crazy dance always worked.

And it still does. Whenever Maria gets low about her art, I threaten to call the Show-Your-Art Guru.

And the mention of it makes her smile still.

Chapter Seventeen

"Obedience and Love"

It was a bitterly cold morning. An icy mist hung over the farm and the woods, and icicles dripping from the trees sparkled in the light. Frieda and I were walking on the path. I stopped to look out at the hills in the distance through an opening in the trees. Frieda paused too, and something out there—a deer maybe, or a fox—caught her eye. The path was still and beautiful, the view in front of us breathtaking. To any passerby, it would have seemed pastoral and sweet, a man and his dog.

Frieda sat down next to me, still fixated on the horizon. I sat down on a big rock as the golden light danced through the trees and the handful of remaining leaves swirled around us. Frieda lay down, and I was shocked when she put her great head on my knee and I saw her big gold-flecked eyes catch the sunlight. I had never seen her so relaxed, especially around me.

"Hey, Frieda," I said, surprised and very quiet. "Thanks, girl." At the sound of my voice, she started and sat up and moved away, growling softly. But still, still . . .

Because I was so close to it, I sometimes didn't realize how much Frieda was changing. It was easier to see how far she had to go. She had been at the farm for more than six months, and we had progressed in our work together. She still could not be with my dogs for any length of time, or come into the farmhouse. She was lying down next to the fence for short periods, but at the first sign of movement, she would lose it and charge the fence. She was beginning to get the idea, but she could not be trusted for any length of time. And she sure didn't look at ease. Her ruff was up, her ears back, her body rigid, all signs of potential aggression.

But she was beginning to listen to me. She was neither obedient nor completely defiant—really, she fell somewhere in the middle. Sometimes, when she was distracted, I thought I saw her tail wagging when I came in. She took beef jerky from my hand now, but I could not get close to her or make her obey. Once in a while, she would sit for me. And she seemed at ease when I visited her in her cozy confinement center, the studio barn.

Frieda was the biggest training challenge of my life with dogs, and I grew a bit every time we worked together. Training a dog challenges us to communicate with a completely unfamiliar mind, one using a totally different kind of language and thinking process.

It was about this time that Annie Sullivan came into my

mind. I remembered her writing on the connection between obedience and learning, and I saw some connection between her approach to teaching the blind and deaf Helen Keller and the way in which I was trying to reach Frieda, who also did not know how to communicate with the world beyond her narrow and troubled universe.

Dogs are not people, and Annie Sullivan's challenge was a lot more groundbreaking than mine, but it also occurred to me that one elemental issue was the same: communicating with an alien and excitable mind that had never been taught how to think and was possessed of a bitter will.

Few people who have heard the story of Annie Sullivan's breaking through to Helen Keller have not been mesmerized by this idea: a blind and deaf mind unable to comprehend, see, or communicate with the world. A mind that seemed to many out of control, beyond reach, willful and rebellious.

It was not until six-year-old Helen threw water on her teacher and was taken outside and had cold water poured onto her hand while the word "water" was tapped out on her other that she connected the feeling with the word, and thus found a gateway to understanding and living in her world.

As she began to teach Helen, she was beset by many difficulties, Sullivan told a newspaper reporter. She said Helen wouldn't yield a point without contesting it to the bitter end. She couldn't coax her or compromise with her. To get Helen to do the simplest thing, she said, it was necessary to resort to force. Sullivan said she saw clearly that it was useless to try to teach Helen language or anything else until Helen learned to obey her. "Obedience and love," she often said, "obedience and love."

Odd, I thought, reading this. If I substituted "Frieda" for "Helen," it fit almost perfectly. Was there relevance for me between Sullivan's approach and Frieda's training?

In our culture—especially in the animal-advocacy community, as well as the political realm—we tend to lock ourselves and others into fixed positions, and we then use these positions to judge one another, often rigidly and with anger.

In politics, we must be "left" or "right" and we must dislike the people on the other side, deemed to be dangerous and ignorant. In dog training, we must adhere to a "pack" theory (dogs are pack animals, and the trainer must be the leader of the pack, asserting his or her authority) or be "positive" (dogs ought only to be trained by reinforcing good behavior, not by focusing on the bad) and if we are not positive, then, by definition, we are "negative," if not abusive or evil. We must always "rescue" a dog if we want one, or we must always get a "bred" dog. The idea that one method sometimes works, and then the other, seems to have gotten lost in the Internet-spawned culture of absolutes. So has the idea of the individual training approach.

Educators know that children are all different, that no single curriculum can fit the needs of all students. But the idea that all dogs are different seems difficult for many people to accept. I had never met a dog like Frieda, and I knew of no single theory that would fit her life or training needs.

In the animal-training culture, gurus prescribe the right ways to train a dog, just as Sullivan faced widespread and quite rigid ideas about communication and education.

Rereading her journals and letters, as well as biographies of her, I saw that Sullivan broke through to her pupil's desperate need to understand by combining great affection (she and Keller adored each other) with an equally powerful demand for obedience and respect. Obedience and love go hand in hand, Sullivan wrote; one cannot exist without the other. I got excited when I read this. This was what I was doing. This was where I needed to go.

Frieda was not a human child, but she was at a turning point in her life. And she did not understand the language of obedience. If she could not learn to obey and understand me, if she could not accept the other dogs and animals—or me, for that matter—then she could not live on the farm.

I was especially interested in Sullivan's revelation that Helen needed to be taken away from her parents, who had always allowed her to do exactly as she pleased. "She has tyrannized everybody," wrote Sullivan; from Helen's mother and father to the servants, no one had ever disputed her will. Like all tyrants, Sullivan said, Helen held tenaciously to her right to do as she pleased.

This also resonated with me, and with the spiritual part of dog training I hold dear. Frieda was a wild and untrained dog, riven with prey drive, but she had also become a brat without boundaries, leaping over fences, charging at and frightening people, roaring when strangers came near, lunging at and bullying other dogs, blowing me and Maria off constantly.

She was a canine tyrant. Nobody could approach the house when Frieda was out; we panicked at the sound of a truck, or the sight of people walking up the road with their dogs a half mile away. For me, training and communicating with a dog begins in just the way Sullivan described. They exist to serve us.

They are not our slaves, but if they live with us and in our world, then they must obey and understand our rules, for our sake and theirs.

Training a dog well has a lot to do with human dignity, although I know of no training book or theory that sees it that way. Annie Sullivan would not abide Helen Keller throwing water at her for the sake of Keller's own dignity and because she herself would not be treated that way. If the two were ever to be able to respect and communicate with each other, then this sort of behavior couldn't continue. Helen's family had treated her much the way Frieda had been treated—as a loved brat who could not really be curtailed or disciplined. As a result, observed Sullivan, Helen had not been able to learn.

In the dog world, the positive-reinforcement trainers teach clarity and patience, using hundreds of repetitions, reinforced by "up" voices, physical and food reinforcement, and praise. Frieda didn't have that much time, and neither did I. And I was not about to beat or club Frieda any more than Annie Sullivan would have manhandled Helen Keller.

Sometimes I think the brutality of the old ways people have viewed animals has been replaced by a different kind of tyranny, a dangerous blend of political correctness, anthropomorphizing, and hypersensitivity. We just seem to find new ways of misunderstanding and exploiting the animals in our lives.

When I walked Frieda by the fence, she would always lunge, jump, and bark as soon as she saw the other dogs, especially Rose, and, teeth bared, she'd begin pulling toward the other side of the road.

One day I reached my foot out and stepped on the leash at a point equidistant from both her lunging body and me. I pulled the leash with my other hand, which drew her head sharply to the ground.

She lunged and barked and growled for several minutes, but there was only one place for her to eventually go, and that was down. When she finally stopped lunging, I said, "Good girl. DOWN!" and I tossed some beef jerky on the ground.

She didn't eat the jerky, but, tired, she did drop down onto the ground, and I pulled the leash tighter to give her even less freedom of movement.

Rose rushed to the fence. I have had Rose since she was eight weeks old, and we have worked together for years in all kinds of situations. I know this dog, and she knows me. Sometimes, on a farm, commands just have to be obeyed and right away. She knows that.

"Hey," I bellowed. "Lie down! Stay down." Rose looked at me, then at Frieda; she emitted a low growl, and then she turned and walked back a few feet and lay down. I knew she would not move, no matter what, and she didn't.

Frieda was shaken. She was growling and whining, but she was looking at me, not at Rose, and she was not moving. I said, "Frieda, come here," in a quieter voice, and Frieda got up and came closer to the fence.

Then I just dropped the leash, kept my foot on it, and stood still for two or three minutes. Frieda stayed down, then got up when I asked her to, and we walked back and forth across the street. I repeated this a half dozen times, whooping with pleasure, praising her and Rose. Rose lay perfectly still, watching. Frieda's ears were up, and so was her tail. She almost pranced across the street, lay down quietly, and looked at me, waiting for a treat, which she took easily.

Her whole demeanor had changed. She was responsive, calm, as if she were having fun. She also seemed startled, awakened in some way, as if, finally, she understood what everybody had been talking to her about, yelling about. Something had gotten through to her. She just seemed brighter, less tense.

When my foot and Frieda's stomach had collided the day I'd gotten her to sit down with Lenore, she'd seemed to view me in a different way. Since then, she'd seemed to notice me more, listen to me, look at me.

As Sullivan wrote of Helen Keller after she refused to let the young girl pour water on her anymore, "the little savage" had learned her first lesson in obedience. It was now Sullivan's job to direct the beautiful intelligence in her pupil. Sullivan's philosophy inspired me. My own savage had learned to pay attention to me, and it was now my task to appreciate the beautiful and proud spirit of this animal and to direct it in ways that would make her safe and able to live in our world. She had never learned to do this, never learned our language, never grasped the meaning of obedience.

One cold Sunday afternoon, I let my dogs out into the front yard, and then I went over to get Frieda. I walked into the studio barn and called her over to me, but in a completely different voice. And with a completely different mind-set.

This was not an aggressive dog. This was not a dog who wished to bite or harm me, and if she had wanted that, she'd had a thousand opportunities to do it. This creature had a huge heart, full of love for the human who finally gave her love in return. This was, I told myself, a beautiful creature, with a wondrous and brave dog soul, and I owed it to her, to Maria, and to myself to use obedience as a gateway to her living in our world, and staying with us, in love, and not in captivity or fear. I would not be blown off, ignored, or mistreated, not by my own dog in my own home.

I have often believed that a dog can sense what is in your head: fear, uncertainty, confusion. And also strength and clarity. I did not want Frieda to be afraid of me any more than Annie Sullivan wanted Helen to fear her. I wanted her to obey me, listen to me, learn from me, and thus love me.

"Frieda. Come," I said in a quiet but firm voice. She ignored me, turning away. I slapped my hand against the wall, and, startled, she turned to me.

"Frieda. Come," I said. I waited a long two or three minutes. "You will come," I said, looking at her, "if I have to stand here all day."

And slowly, sniffing the ground, looking away, she did come over to me, or at least within a few feet, her ears back, watching me warily.

I picked a leash up off the rack where Maria kept them, and I leaned over to snap it over Frieda's collar. She growled and then took my wrist in her mouth, as a warning. Again, she did not bite me. I flexed the first three fingers of my other hand and flicked them, nail side to her, against the tip of her nose as hard as I could. She started a bit, and then let go of my wrist. My confidence grew. If I could do that, I could progress quickly.

"No," I said in a new and much louder voice. "You will never put your mouth on me again. Never." And she stayed still as I slipped the leash to her collar, and she quite meekly walked alongside me, out the door and across the street to where my dogs were lying. I tossed her some beef jerky, which she ate hungrily.

For me, the issue came down to this: What is the true nature of love? Is it really love to see the creatures in our care as too fragile and damaged to learn how to live safely in our world? To take their abuse from them and use it as an excuse to leave them stranded in our world?

Or does love involve some measure of iron will and discipline to make sure that the animals (and people) we are responsible for learn how to live in the world? To be safe and not harm themselves, or any other living things?

I am not only the owner of dogs and sheep and donkeys, I am also a father, and I remember asking this same question a million times as the culture around me seemed to turn away from firmness, discipline, and obedience as appropriate learning tools.

I am no hard-ass, either as a parent or a dog lover, but it's perhaps not surprising that disciplining dogs has become as unacceptable as disciplining kids. I remember teachers telling me how frustrated they were at the growing numbers of parents who insisted that whatever went wrong in school was the teacher's fault, not their own responsibility or their children's.

I was determined not to treat Frieda as the sad and abandoned rescue creature many people talked of when they met or heard of her. I didn't want to see her like that, and I didn't want her to become that. Maria, always honest, always self-analytical, conceded that she'd never really tried to change Frieda because she didn't know how and because she didn't want to inflict one iota of further suffering on this animal she loves.

Sullivan inspired me to separate myself from that sentiment, as it is not the stance of a teacher. Or a trainer. Like Keller, Frieda was going to either learn to live in the world or vanish into a dark place. I was pretty determined about which course she was going to take.

And that, I was coming to see, was perhaps the purest kind of love.

Frieda and I worked alone together every morning just after sunup, after Maria went to work. She no longer resisted my leashing her, and this act of submission was important, I knew. We worked together every day for two or three weeks. I told Maria nothing about this training, as I wanted to surprise her.

One day, after Maria came home, I invited her out in the yard and asked her to stand on the porch.

I went across the street, into the studio barn, and called Frieda out of her crate. She came to me, growling halfheartedly as I leashed her up. I tossed her a liver treat, which she devoured.

I gave her a pep talk: "Hey, Frieda, we're going out to the yard and you are going to sit and lie down with the other dogs. Maria will be watching, and this will be a surprise for her. She will be very happy. This will be a huge step for you. . . . So this is going to work, right?"

I took a deep breath and pushed aside the thoughts of Frieda eating Lenore or brawling with Rose. If this was going to work, I had to visualize Frieda sitting calmly with the other dogs; I had to project confidence.

As we walked out, I gave Frieda a sharper than usual tug on her leash to make sure I had her attention, and I said, "Hey!" She walked alongside me, eager, as always, to take a walk.

Maria, standing across the road on the farmhouse porch, was watching us closely. She was already surprised, as she had not seen Frieda walk like that with me. As we approached the road, Frieda saw the other dogs, who were all sitting in the yard, watching us; Rose was quiet. Frieda stiffened.

"Down. Now," I said, quietly but very confidently, and Frieda whined a bit, growled a bit, and then dropped down.

"Lie down" is one of the most important commands, because it not only puts the dog in a calming and submissive position but also greatly reduces the likelihood of trouble, such as running off or fighting. The dog is essentially saying, "I am submitting to you; I am in a submissive position." Dogs rarely go off to fight or make trouble from that position, if they are trained to hold it, and it reinforces the idea that they are obeying the person giving them the command. For a fiercely dominant dog like Frieda, that is seminal, as important to our training as Helen Keller's submission to Annie Sullivan's pouring water on her hand.

I heard Maria say, "Wow" from the porch, and then I put my finger to my lips to ask for quiet, as I didn't want to distract Frieda, who always wanted to know where Maria was.

I told Frieda to "heel," and we walked across the road. I asked her to lie down again, and again, every few feet until we got to the gate. I was eager for Maria's response, but I didn't want to take my eyes off Frieda, and I wanted her to know that

I was paying attention to her. I dropped some liver treats on the ground, and she scarfed them up. She was a bit stiff, very alert. I yelled to my dogs to "get back" and they all did, except for Lenore, of course, who was at the gate wagging her tail. I thought that was good, a possible relaxing signal for Frieda as well as for Rose and Izzy. Although Izzy is not a fighter, not very dominant, he has little patience for loud or pushy dogs, and I could easily imagine a free-for-all if things got out of hand.

Now I could see Maria grinning from ear to ear, but also suddenly concerned as we approached the gate rather than continuing on to the rear of the farmhouse. "You're not bringing her into the yard, are you?" she said, worried.

The last time she had seen Frieda near the fence, it had been an ugly and loud scene: dogs barking, charging, growling.

I said we were coming in, and I unlatched the gate and had Frieda lie down. She was very intense, very alert, but quiet.

Then I walked her into the yard, about five or ten feet. Other than Lenore, still wagging her tail, who came over to lick Frieda on the nose, none of the other dogs had moved. Izzy was looking away, toward the road. Rose was locked on, watching Frieda intently.

I told Frieda to lie down, and then I dropped the leash. Maria gasped; I looked over and thought she was going to faint. I stepped back a few feet and told everyone to "stay," reinforcing this with hand signals. I dropped some liver treats in front of Frieda and then walked over and gave some to Izzy, Rose, and then Lenore, whom I had called over nearer to the other dogs.

I felt like I was in control, and maybe that was why Frieda seemed in control. I stayed between her and them and listened to the happy sound of crunching. There was no growling or stiffness. Izzy looked away, across the valley. Rose ate one treat and then turned her attention to the sheep, which she could see across the meadow. Lenore picked up a twig and chewed on it, alert for more liver treats, her tail wagging.

For Maria and me, crossing the fence line was a big deal. But perhaps it was not such a big deal for the dogs. Rose and Frieda each understood the importance of boundaries, especially Frieda, who had been trained to guard fences. But even though Frieda had been spending her days and nights in the studio barn, all of the dogs were aware of one another, could see, hear, and smell each other. Once they were all on the same side of the fence, they didn't seem to see it as all that big a deal.

I had noticed that Frieda's biggest problems were with boundaries. She had, of course, been trained as a guard dog, taught to protect the boundaries of the auto body shop. And she had done that. But I was beginning to realize that when she had no boundaries, she was much calmer. She was off the clock and could relax. Dogs, like horses and donkeys, are pack animals. They like to hang around with other dogs. By walking Frieda inside the fence, I had removed her boundary—she had nothing to guard. The other dogs were with her, not trying to come into her space. It was a significant discovery, a big step in our training, and in Frieda's entry into the life of the farm. Suddenly, these were not strange dogs she was trying to keep out; they were dogs on the same side of the fence. A big difference, I could tell.

In time, I wondered if Frieda might not see the dogs as something to protect, rather than something to drive off. Maybe she would see me that way, too.

After five minutes, at the end of which all of the dogs were sitting quietly, watching me or staring out at nothing in particular, Maria came running off the porch, threw her arms around me, and then dropped down to hug Frieda, who rolled over onto her back in delight to get her belly scratched.

It always brought me up short to see Maria and Frieda together, touched my heart only in the way the connections between people and animals can. Maria was Frieda's world. She never took her eyes off her; the two of them would just collapse into each other's lives. Whatever happened to either of them, these two had weathered storms together, a fusion of the heart, two species coming together in a dance of loyalty and love.

Maria's emotions are much closer to the surface than mine, and she cries so often that it sometimes embarrasses her. Sitting next to Frieda, she cried again. She had despaired, she said, of seeing Frieda in the yard. I was not surprised by her tears. Every night before we went to bed, Maria would wonder about Frieda: Was she lonely? Was she warm enough? Did she have enough to eat? Was she all right there? Many nights, she had to go check on her before she could go to sleep. It was clear how difficult it was for her to leave Frieda over in the studio barn.

"Thank you, thank you," Maria said. "I never thought this would happen." And she gave me a deep and loving kiss, positive reinforcement for the trainer.

I was proud of myself, beaming. I leaned over and scratched Frieda under the chin, and she forgot to growl or snap at me. For a few seconds, anyway.

I didn't tell Maria that I was determined to have Frieda living in the house by Christmas, a couple of months away. She would not have believed me. But now that Frieda and I were beginning to communicate, anything might be possible.

Chapter Eighteen

The Christmas Miracle

Each day, Frieda and I walked in the woods. We did obedience lessons. We worked on "sit" and "stay" all over the farm. Despite some growling and stiffening, she let me put a leash on her. She accepted me more. Sometimes she would lie down outside the fence near the other dogs. Sometimes not. Yet I also felt a growing tide of frustration and confusion. When she could find a way, she would run off, disappear for hours, come back with blood on her paws and snout.

Loud truck engines, people on bikes, dog walkers, and delivery people continued to drive her berserk. She broke through the screen in the studio barn twice, once terrifying a kid walking to the school bus. She tried to get over the fence at the donkeys. She did get over the fence once when a motorcycle went by. Luckily, no one was hurt.

The truth was, we were stuck. We had come far, but we were not moving farther. My Christmas plan for bringing Frieda into the house seemed remote, at best. She was still a wild dog in many ways. And I was running out of training tricks.

It was one of those truly biblical upstate winter nights. The temperature was well below zero, and an arctic wind was howling through the bare trees and blowing the deep snow-drifts around. The sheep and donkeys were huddled in the barn, the dogs in their various beds and corners, and it seemed as if we were living at the end of the earth. I guess, in many ways, we were.

Maria has the gift of sleeping through almost anything, while almost anything will wake me up and keep me up. I woke up that night because something—an icicle, a tree limb—had blown into one of the downstairs windows and made a chilling thump. I heard the wind shrieking, and then I thought I heard another sound, something mournful and piercing: a deep and lonely cry, clearly a howl.

I sat up, wondering if some animal was dying out there, or if some coyote or wolf had come to stalk the sheep on this awful night. Moving slowly, so as not to waken Maria, I went to the window and cocked my ear, and I realized soon enough that the howl was coming from the studio barn, just across the road. It was almost surely Frieda howling. I put on my glasses and peered into the darkness. I could see that the squall had forced the door to the barn open, and the wind and snow had to be blowing in on her.

I pulled on jeans and a sweatshirt and went downstairs, got into my boots and a jacket, and ran outside—not realizing that Rose had slipped out behind me in the dark, as she always does—every single time—when there is trouble. Outside, the cold was so intense that it seemed it would pierce my lungs. I had to take short, quick breaths.

There was a foot of snow on the ground, and the wind shrieked in bursts. I felt for any people or animals out that night. When I crossed the street, I froze—it was then that I was aware of Rose by my side—and I heard the howl again, sorrowful and deep, a sound so sad that I forgot the cold. Frieda was sitting by the open door, calling out.

I raced across the road. I was so affected by this sound—I didn't want Maria to hear it, as she would be stricken—that I didn't really even think about Rose, and as we approached the studio barn, Frieda got up, moving right for Rose's throat.

Rose stood her ground, growling.

It is curious, but I rarely panic around the animals, even in situations like this one. Rose and I had been through so much together on the farm that I simply reacted, calling on instincts I never knew were there. In a strange way, I felt as comfortable working with animals, even in crises, as I did sitting at my computer.

I took a breath and made sure I was calm and sounded calm. I simply said, "No." After a few seconds, Frieda backed up and she and Rose just looked at each other, sniffed the air around each other, and it seemed to me that something professional passed between them, some respect and understanding.

This was not a time to hurt each other, and they both seemed to understand that.

Frieda turned and went back into the studio barn, and I told Rose to stay. I knew she would.

I got Frieda back into her crate, stoked up the fire, which was still going, and swept the snow out of the doorway. Before I left, Frieda looked at me in a very different and penetrating way. "I hear you," I said, and I did.

I wondered if Frieda had howled like that before, or if the storm and the wind made her anxious or lonely in a new and different way. I wondered if she had just had enough of listening to the sounds from the house, of Maria and me talking to each other, of the dogs barking and moving around. Had had enough of her own frenzy and confusion, of her loneliness. Frieda had had a tough life, and maybe she was sick of that tough life and wanted some time inside a warm house with the person she loved more than life itself.

I came into the house, warmed my hands in hot water, stomped the snow off my boots.

A few minutes later, I was back in bed, Rose curled by the foot of it, still watching over me. I drifted off to sleep, and at some point that night, I had the following dream:

I was hiking through the woods and Frieda was walking alongside me, hidden from me, although I was aware of her presence.

We walked for hours and hours, to the deepest and most remote part of the forest. It seemed as if I had walked forever, across mead-

ows and over rocks and through so many dark shadows, but finally I came into a clearing, and in the moonlight Frieda was sitting there, waiting for me, looking at me.

I was tired, but she was not. She looked beautiful in the moonlight, her black-and-brown coat shiny and smooth. Her big brown eyes were as large as saucers and looked yellow and luminous in the light of the moon. She was a powerful sight, the ur-dog, out in the wild.

We looked at each other for the longest time, and then I broke the silence and said, "I don't know what to do with you. I love you and want to live with you, but I am sad and frustrated. I've tried everything I can think of, but what else can I do? What do you want from me?"

And then, without moving her lips or snout, without making a sound, Frieda spoke to me.

"Trust me," she said.

And then I woke up.

Finally, I understood what I needed to do, what Frieda wanted from me. It was so simple that I had missed it, so easy that I couldn't help looking over and around it, as people are wont to do with dogs.

Dogs, in one way or another, have been talking to people for thousands of years, and people have been talking back. It was not really all that surprising that Frieda had a message for me, only that it had taken me so long to listen.

We spend hundreds—thousands—of dollars and hours seeking out the teachings of experts when the answers, of course, are often right under our noses. We are just too closed up and distracted to see them. Frieda was asking me for a second chance, just as life had offered me a second chance. Now, I sensed, she wanted hers. Maria and I had decided to go for ours, to take it, and Frieda, with her exquisitely honed instincts for survival and adaptation, knew on some level that she had to either come along or stay in what for her had to be a difficult place, shut off in the studio barn, unable to protect her favorite person.

So that was it. We all wanted to change. Maria and I had decided to trust each other. Frieda wanted in. Could it be that simple? Could it be anything else?

The Sunday before Christmas, just before Maria came home from work, I went to the studio barn and opened Frieda's crate. Confidently and with trust, I reached down and clipped the leash to her collar.

She looked up at me, almost as if to say, "What took you so long?" and I said, "Let's go." And that's the thing with fear and dogs: it isn't about them; it's about you. I had always approached her as if we couldn't do it, as if I didn't trust her. Maria had done the same thing. Frieda was the wild dog, the crazy dog, the unpredictable and scary dog. That was what we saw in her, so that was what she saw reflected in us.

Now I was showing her something else, another feeling.

I was trusting her.

We crossed the road; it was cold but not snowing. I said nothing. I was worried about Rose and the other dogs, but I brushed that away. I had to trust Frieda. She had asked for it—I totally believed that—and I was offering it. Or trying to.

We got to the door, and I heard some barking and scuffling as Rose, Izzy, and Lenore rushed up to see who was there. I opened the door and yelled, "Get back," but that was foolish, and, of course, they did not.

Frieda balked a bit, then growled, and then we were inside the farmhouse, for the first time in Frieda's life. I took a deep breath and dropped the leash.

Rose and Izzy stiffened, and so did Frieda. Lenore rushed up and licked Frieda on the nose, coming between her and the border collies. I moved into the next room, grabbed a bucket of smelly liver treats. I yelled, "Treat!" and in a flash, all four dogs were on me and grabbing their snacks. They seemed to have forgotten one another.

People always overlook how adaptable dogs are, how easily they change and move along in life. It is perhaps their most enduring trait and survival skill, yet we often think they are as complex and confused as we are and forget to trust them to figure out life and deal with one another.

I got out four bowls and filled them with kibble. Rose's and Izzy's went in the kitchen; I placed Frieda's and Lenore's out in the hallway.

They ate without incident, all of them hungry. Then I put Frieda back on a leash and we all went outside together, down the path. The four dogs paid little or no attention to one another. At one point, Rose and Frieda engaged in a bit of butt sniffing, and that was good.

We all came back into the house together, and I was Santa for dogs that afternoon, dispensing lots of treats. Then I called

Frieda over to me and sat down in the living room. I was nervous, but then I told myself to settle down, and I did.

Frieda zoned in on the mat in front of the woodstove as if she had been waiting for it all of her arthritic life, and I think she had. She lay down, curled up, and went to sleep. Rose vanished into one of her corners. Lenore curled up next to Frieda and started snoring. Izzy disappeared behind the sofa.

I couldn't believe what I was seeing. It seemed as if they had all done this a thousand times, each dog in its own spot.

I started reading, staying vigilant. A few minutes later, I heard Maria's car come up the driveway, and so did Frieda and the other dogs.

They all got up and rushed to the back door, which opened; a moment later, I heard a shout from Maria.

"Frieda!" she said. "My God, you're in the house." There was some silence, and then Maria rushed into the living room and threw her arms around me.

I have to tell you, this was one of the sweetest and most memorable moments of my life. I've never felt bigger or better than I did as Maria threw her arms around me and four dogs danced and circled around her, tails wagging.

Frieda pushed her way up to me, in front of Maria, forgetting for a moment to be remote and vigilant, and she put her head on my knee and wagged her tail. I smiled.

"I can't believe it," Maria said. "Frieda is in the house! How did you do it? I never thought this would happen."

"All right, dogs," I yelled, "settle down. Leave us alone!" Frieda ran to the dog bed by the stove, just ahead of Lenore. Lenore jumped up onto the sofa, where she is usually forbidden to go. Izzy and Rose disappeared.

It seemed as if it had always been this way, had been what all of the dogs wanted. They'd simply been waiting for me to make it happen.

Maria went over to Frieda and lay down on the floor, wrapping her arms around her big protector. Frieda looked more content than I had ever seen her. She sighed and melted into Maria's arms. The world seemed very right to me.

There was only one thing I could say to Maria.

"Merry Christmas."

After that, things changed. Trusting Frieda—perhaps the only thing I had never really thought of doing—seemed to unlock her better side, open up her great heart. The Frieda I was now getting to know was a lot of fun—smart, playful, curious.

She still had her issues, and plenty of them: she does not love strange men, and she does not like to be touched by anyone but me and Maria. Her changes came in increments—slowly, but steadily and visibly, day by day.

Maria (with Frieda at her side) was making her fiber arts business work. Frieda even became part of the logo for Full Moon Fiber Art. In the morning, Maria and Frieda would trot over to the studio barn together, and Frieda would sit in her open crate and watch Maria quietly all day long, pausing only to growl and rumble at the mail carrier or the UPS driver.

Maria tried bringing the other dogs over to the studio barn once in a while, but it didn't pan out. Frieda was the only one who didn't bother Maria while she was working or step on the fabric she laid out on the floor. Frieda was content just to be watching over Maria, her life's work. And she was even happier, at the end of the day, to trot with her back to the farmhouse, where she had scoped out and cornered some of the best spots. She had a bed up in Maria's office on the second floor. She had another bed in front of the woodstove in the winter. In warm weather, she liked the shady corner of the family room at the end of the farmhouse.

Frieda enjoyed her new comforts, and none of the other dogs ever beat her to the roaring woodstove on cold nights. When we went to bed, Frieda followed us and took up guard duty. It's good sleeping when you know Frieda is there keeping an eye on things. You feel safe.

It turns out that Frieda loves being a pack dog and had no issues of any kind with the other dogs. She plays with Lenore. She dozes next to Izzy. She and Rose, both working girls, always sit next to each other at the dog fence or on the lawn. They both love to stare for hours at the road.

Another big development: more and more, Frieda likes to be with me when I write. When Maria heads off to the studio barn, Frieda is given a choice: go with her or stay with me. Many mornings, she looks at both of us and heads for the door to my study, where she can command a clear view of all approaches to the farm and to me.

She crosses her legs and lowers her head, but she rarely sleeps. She watches. As cars and trucks pass, she growls. If somebody pulls into the driveway, she is on her feet, fur up, barking, moving in front of me. Oddly enough, this has helped me tremendously in my work. I have significant concentration problems, as Maria will testify. My mind is always racing. Many things distract me, and I hate to be bothered when I am writing. Frieda makes me feel secure, helps me focus my energy in the right place. And it is important to say this: Frieda makes a lot of noise, but she has never harmed anyone. I still fear for the animals in the woods, but she doesn't get near them anymore.

I trust Frieda.

I used to dread the thought of Frieda living in the same house as me. I now silently hope she chooses me every morning. More and more, she does.

Maria restored one of our barns, the pig barn, and turned it into an art gallery, a lifelong dream of hers. There, she shows the work of talented local artists, including herself. The first show was a huge success—more than one thousand people came. On the first day, there was an artists' reception, and I was invited to say a few words about the commitment Maria and I felt to encourage artists and find ways to show and sell art in a struggling economy.

Before my talk, as the barn filled up with people, I excused myself briefly and told Maria I had to get something from the house. I walked into an upstairs room where Frieda had been crated. She looked up at me as I approached the crate, and I remembered those days when I would walk into the studio barn, drop some beef jerky, and run.

"Listen, girl," I said, opening the crate. "The days when you are hidden away are gone. We're going to see your mom in the pig barn. Watch yourself and don't give me any reason to regret this. I trust you—mostly." Frieda was watching me intently with her big brown beautiful eyes. These eyes had seen a lot, been through a lot, understood a lot, I now knew.

I do not believe Frieda understood my words, but I believe she got the drift. I put the leash on her, and we walked out the back door, right into the middle of a crowd of hundreds of people. She seemed to be quite at home, strutting alongside me as if we were in a parade. I asked people not to touch her, and most didn't, although a couple of people did reach out their hands, and she winced and pulled back. Clearly, she did not feel safe being touched around the neck.

But there were many oohs and aahs. Frieda had not been seen by many people outside our circle of friends, and I was struck by how comfortable she was. She was curious, sniffing the ground, lifting her head to look for Maria.

We walked through the crowds and into the pig barn, and I was happy to see Maria's shocked and delighted smile. I thought I saw a few tears as well. I dropped the leash and Frieda ran over to Maria, pressed her head against her knee, and then turned, looked for me, and came over to my side.

I told her to lie down, which she did, and I gave my talk. Frieda lay her head on the ground and didn't move. We both got a huge ovation when we left—I didn't want to push my luck—and as we made our way back down the driveway and into the house, there was no prouder dad in the world than me.

Once inside, I took off the leash, dropped to the ground, kissed Frieda on the nose—she loved it—and tossed some treats into her crate.

A few months later, I brought Frieda to a reading at a local bookstore. There were perhaps forty people in the store. I came in with her, and she crawled right under the table and went to sleep. I talked for half an hour, took questions, and signed a few books. When I was done, Frieda extricated herself from under the table and followed me outside and into the car. I didn't think much about it. Up to that point, she'd been the only one of my dogs that had never been to a public reading. Now there was really nothing that the other dogs did that she didn't do.

With one big exception: herding sheep. I still didn't have the guts for that. Maybe one day.

Frieda has steadily and smoothly been woven into the fabric of our lives. When we first got her, she took off after Mother the barn cat and nearly killed her. Now she walks out every morning to her dog fence while Mother eats her morning snack. They walk right past each other. The sheep come right up to her fence to graze, and she barely looks up at them.

But for me, the most touching and compelling sign of her evolution came just recently, on a fall day, while I was sitting on the enclosed porch, writing. Frieda was beside me. The chickens—the rooster Winston III and his two hens—were walking on the driveway near the road, searching for bugs and worms. I heard some alarmed clucking and barking. A local dog had come up the road from town and was heading straight for the chickens.

Winston took off on a suicide run, puffing himself up and charging down the driveway toward the dog, who was closing rapidly on the chickens. The rooster would not have gotten far.

I jumped up, called for Frieda—she had spotted the dog and was growling—and rushed her to the porch door and opened it. Had I thought about it, I would not have sent her off running near the chickens. But I didn't have time to think about it. She was the guard dog, and I needed her.

Frieda tore across the yard and, without even skipping a beat, sailed right over the wooden fence, and landed directly in front of the dog, an ill-tempered creature whose owners were not much nicer.

Frieda showed her impressive teeth and charged the dog just as Winston arrived, squawking and flapping his wings. It occurred to me then that Winston's chances of surviving this standoff were now much worse than they had been. The dog didn't waste much time considering things; he turned and ran back down the road. Frieda chased him only so far as the driveway ended and then, to my amazement, stopped and turned to look at me—and then Winston.

"No!" I yelled, rushing across the yard. But then I stopped. Frieda was lying down. The two hens were pecking through the grass ten feet from her. They seemed to trust her absolutely. Did they know, I wondered, that she had saved them?

Winston III soon joined them, and by the time I got there, the four of them were hanging out together in a peaceful and pastoral scene.

It was then, perhaps, that I realized that Frieda wasn't just protecting me and Maria. She was protecting the farm and all of the things on it, material and animal. Frieda had been living with the chickens around for months. They were now under her care.

And you know what? That is a good place to be in this world.

I rushed to tell Maria this news, and she ran over to give Frieda a hug. Frieda seemed quite pleased with herself.

As I walked away, I was very happy to hear her say, "Oh, Frieda, we got to a better place, didn't we? We got to a better place."

All of us.

Chapter Nineteen

My Happy Ending

> I call heaven and earth to record this
> day against you, that I have set before
> you life and death, blessing and curs-
> ing: therefore choose life, that both
> thou and thy seed may live.
>
> —*Deuteronomy 30:19*

After Maria had finally succumbed to my persistent proposals, I vacillated between thinking she'd just gotten tired of saying no and thinking, Well, maybe she does love me. There was only one way to find out, and we were under way.

The truth is, I'd never really doubted that Maria would say

yes. We loved each other, loved being together so much that there just wasn't much of a reason for us not to get married. I had told Maria that she needed to own half the farm in order to feel as if she lived there. And should anything go wrong with us, she needed to have something to take with her. I didn't understand people who lived together and professed to love each other but kept their possessions separate. That kind of holding back never jibed with me.

We both laughed about our "sliding" toward a decision. "We'll have fun," I said, and we both knew that was true. I do remember Maria saying that if I turned out to be a controlling jerk, like the men many of her friends were married to, she would really be pissed.

I said if that happened, she should walk away, no hard feelings.

We didn't talk about it much after that; we just started planning. We wanted to be married in a Quaker-style ceremony in a local meetinghouse, but that didn't work out—the elders weren't sure about the dogs. So we settled on the big barn: our own church, our own cathedral.

Maria and I had, at long last, decided to be happy. To go for it. To take the leap of faith. To live our lives. To follow what we both believed was sacred in life, the creative sparks inside us, to heed the inner voices and bring some light into the world. We knew so many people who accepted unhappiness in their lives, and we had ourselves been so unhappy. Our vow was to not end our days that way but to take each other's hand and heart and walk to a better place.

My daughter, of course, saw it differently, at least at first. In her eyes, my divorce had torn the family apart and caused much pain and sorrow. She was good and brave to hold my ring for me that day. I know it cost her.

There was no one in the world I would rather have had standing alongside me that day than my daughter.

To be honest, I remember only fragments of our wedding day. I was in shock, overcome by a mixture of love, joy, and disbelief.

I remember that it was raining. Maria wore a red dress, in her artsy gypsy style. I wore chinos, a blue sweater vest, and brown shoes. We put floral wreaths on the donkeys, Lulu and Fanny, and I remember how the two of them vanished into the pasture once the crowd began arriving.

I remember all the people clustering around me, and Reverend Mary Muncil taking us into the living room and closing the door so we could have some peace and gather ourselves. A van filled with food pulled up, and bottles of wine and cakes were set out on tables on the porch.

Every few minutes, Maria and I grabbed each other's hands and just held on. "Why didn't we just go to city hall?" I hissed, and she said she didn't know, but of course, we were both very happy to be on the farm. It was the perfect place for us to be married. Besides, in West Hebron, New York, there is no city hall.

The only sad note was poor Frieda, who, on this most important day, was locked up in her crate in the studio barn. I'd argued for days that she be present at the ceremony, that I should walk her in and take responsibility for her, but Maria, wiser and more clearheaded than me, vetoed this. She didn't want the day marked by any trouble, not for Frieda, not for us.

I remember members of my family, most of whom I had not seen or spoken with in years, arriving and introducing themselves, and my struggling to get comfortable with them, as they seemed so familiar with me, yet were not.

I remember walking out into the meadow with Rose, where we could not be seen, and thanking her for her loyalty and love and great work, which had helped get me through my years alone on the farm. "You will not be shunted aside," I promised her. "I still need you."

I remember when Chris Barrett, a friend we had hired to help out that morning, came to the back door and said they were ready for us. I took a deep breath, reminding myself not to blow it. Walking out into the rain, I heard the pianist playing "Here Comes the Sun" on a digital piano.

I remember calling the dogs and Rose, Lenore, and Izzy rushing ahead of us.

I remember people speaking to us, toasting us, and wishing us well. I do not remember what most of them said. I was looking at Maria, hanging on to her hand for dear life, soaking up her sweet smile, her tears, the love that shone in her eyes. I remember Reverend Mary reminding us and the whole gathering that we had chosen life, and I remember crying when I heard that, because it was so true.

As is typical of me, I never kept any copies of my wedding vows. I am not a man who dwells in the past much. Life, for me, is a wheel that moves forward and carries me along with it. What I remember is that during the "vow" portion of the ceremony, I told Maria that I was a storyteller and she was my happy ending. That drew a lot of oohs and aahs from the assembled guests. As a writer, I am sensitive to reviews, and I could feel the chord I struck in those assembled.

When our friend Mary pronounced us husband and wife, Maria and I looked at each other and, without words, understood the power and the glory of what we were doing.

We chose life. That's what we were about. That's why we were there, in that barn that rainy and muggy day, one of the happiest of my life.

We chose life.

We choose it still, every hour of every day, to the end.

About one hundred people had crowded into the cavernous upper story of the big barn, where hay and grain had been stored, cows had been milked, and animals had been slaughtered, all in the distant past. The old barn, built before the Civil War, had seen a lot of history, but nothing like this. Everybody was clean, sweet-smelling, and in city clothes.

Maria had artistically placed flowerpots around, and her nieces and nephews sat up on the hay bales, where the barn cats sleep. A local deli brought in some pies and sandwiches—Lenore, crafty as ever, managed to eat a whole pie. But there was no turning the barn into the kind of dining room you would find at a fancy inn. Animals had been in that barn for more than a hundred and fifty years, and you could tell. Still, it was simple and beautiful.

When it came time for Emma to give her "best man's" speech, she quoted from Woody Allen's monologue at the end of the movie *Annie Hall*:

"This guy goes to a psychiatrist and says, 'Doc, my brother's crazy: he thinks he's a chicken.' And the doctor says, 'Well, why don't you turn him in?' The guy says, 'I would, but I need the eggs.'"

Most people in the barn, Emma noted, had probably been through some rough times with romance. "I think it's probably very reasonable to get discouraged," she said. "But reason isn't everything. I'm glad that my dad and Maria were irrational enough to keep looking for love, and so glad that they found it."

And I was so glad that she could see that and say it.

During one painful session with a therapist, I had said I feared that my daughter and I would be disconnected from each other's lives for good, and she'd looked up at me, taken off her glasses, and said calmly, but with emphasis:

"You gave your daughter the greatest gift anyone could possibly give. You showed her that you can be happy."

Sometimes, when I think of that, I still go into the barn by myself, and I stand by the big old window where Mary pronounced us husband and wife, and I just cry. I remember the life I left behind—the fear and loneliness, the confusion and anger. I think of those things as ghosts and spirits I put to rest in the barn that day.

After the ceremony, my editor and I walked up the hillside to watch Rose move the sheep around. Mary had urged me to take a second and consider the wedding, to absorb the moment, and so, standing up on that hillside, I did. I could see Maria down below talking to her family, could see people milling around the driveway, and I felt for a moment that I had been transported out of my life and was watching a movie of it. I could not quite recollect how I had gotten from there to here.

What came to my mind was love, and its power.

If you have experienced it, I thought, it can never be taken away. To those few people who warned me about getting married again, and so quickly, all I can say is that when you have really known love, it doesn't matter if you lose it. That would be sad, of course, but at least you would know what it is.

And if you love fairy tales, I thought, standing up on that hill, then you know there is almost always a sad part to them, too, and that is true of Maria and me as well. The only thing that separates us, the one thing we cannot and never will share, is this: I am getting old, and she is not yet.

I am closer to the end. She will almost surely have to bear the loss of me, and although the opposite could be true, it is not, I think, likely.

The biggest fight we have had in our time together was over life insurance. I wanted to get some, and she didn't want me to. We fought about it for months. It wasn't us, she said, we didn't need it, and I couldn't imagine why she was so opposed to it. And then, one day, I saw clearly what was happening. She could not bear to think of me dying. The idea that she might benefit from my death was deeply upsetting to her. So I just went ahead and got some without telling her.

The night before the wedding, as we were lying in bed for the last time as single people, she turned to me and said, "I'm so happy. I feel like I've just been given another chance at life." "Me too," I answered, but I did not let her see my eyes tear up as I thought of all the time we'd lost and the life we might have had together, the children we might have raised, the things we might have done.

I tried to push these thoughts away. After all, I might very well live a good long time. And I was learning every day how to age well, and to one day die well. To be a true and faithful lover and friend. And now I had a good reason to work even harder at that.

Still, as we held each other that last time before becoming husband and wife, I wondered if Maria would still love me when I got older, and my body started to fall apart, and loving me became a chore. I let those words slip from my mouth, and Maria turned and put a finger to my lips and said, "Sssssssssh, please don't ever say that again." I promised her I wouldn't.

"Let's go get married," she said.

And we did. . . .

Epilogue

Frieda in Autumn
September 2012

The schoolkids who walk on the road call her the "big brown dog," and they have come to terms with her. A couple of years ago, she would roar at them and charge at the fence, scaring them to death. One time, she even jumped the fence and landed in front of a boy, who simply froze in terror. But once there, she wasn't quite sure what to do with herself. She barked a few times, until I rushed over and yelled at her to get away. She did.

Country kids seem to know dogs like Frieda, and they don't take her all that seriously. They have good instincts. In the years we have been with Frieda, she has never bitten or harmed anyone on two legs. Her bark is, in fact, much worse than her bite, although her bark is pretty impressive.

Things are different now, on our road. The kids come by on their way to school, sometimes on their bikes, and Frieda seems to scarcely notice them. If they are pulling a wagon or riding furiously, she might let off an indignant growl. It is, after all, her yard, her road, her farmhouse. Sometimes they even wave at her, and, ever imperious, she looks away. Frieda has mellowed and found her place.

Not so many people are afraid of her these days, except maybe the UPS guy, who challenges her boundaries regularly and delivers his packages to Maria across the road if he sees Frieda in the yard. Or Teddy, the cocky little poodle, who still dares to walk by her farm every morning and night.

Frieda is in her autumn.

Her muzzle is gray, her coat drying out, her legs getting lame. She has found her spot: right under the big old maple in the corner of the farmhouse yard. Frieda is a sun worshipper, like her human, Maria, and even in the hottest weather she likes to soak in the rays, as if she is storing them up for dark and cold times. She is learning how to let some things go—loud trucks, go-carts, motorcycles; she'll watch as they pass without trying to stop them. She lets the other dogs take her treats right out of her mouth and even challenges them to play once in a while.

Frieda and I have found common ground. The surprise for me is that so many more things connect us than separate us these days:

We both love Maria and want to protect her.

We both love to walk on the path in the woods together.

We both have sore knees and a touch of arthritis, and we are happier to sit down on our soft sofas and dog beds than before. We both love the woodstove and want to be near it.

We have both learned that there are things in the world we can control and things in the world we can't control. And a meaningful life for both of us is, in some ways, knowing the difference.

We have made that soul connection that some lucky people and dogs make. I love Frieda. Frieda loves me. Like a troubled adolescent who couldn't stand her dad, she has discovered that there are some things about me that are worthwhile.

At one time or another, Frieda tried to maim or kill every creature on the farm—donkeys, barn cats, chickens, other dogs. That is no longer so. Frieda now sees the whole farm and all of its denizens as hers. She guards all of us. We are all under her vigilant care, scrupulously protected from loud engines, impertinent dogs, noisy boys.

We still do our training, but it is fairly pro forma now, as Frieda's muzzle grays and her feet tire. Mostly, she comes when called, quiets when told, lies down on command. Frieda has settled in, and I don't want to bother her much. We have reached that mystical point in the life of a man and a dog where we have come to love and accept each other, and we know that nothing more is going to change much, or needs to.

Sometimes, when Frieda stares out into the woods, into the

valley, I like to imagine that she is remembering the old days—hunting chipmunks and rabbits, dodging bears, digging warm and dry holes for herself, running free in the forest, hiding from dogcatchers, skirting traps, avoiding bait and tricks. I do not imagine that these are bad memories for Frieda; quite the opposite. I think they were, in some ways, the best days of her remarkable life. She got to live the life of a dog, in every sense.

I wonder if Frieda recalls her babies, thinks of them, if her powerful instincts bring them into her consciousness. I don't know. Sometimes I think she looks mournful and reflective, but that is almost surely a projection of mine.

Frieda has taken on another task I love: she is now my writing dog, something she used to do occasionally but has now made a focal point of her work. As I write this, she is sitting by my office, paws crossed, guarding the door and the hallway. She has picked up on the idea of keeping things away from me while I work—except for Maria—and it is amazing how much she helps me concentrate on my prose. I love having a dog who guards me. I love having a writing dog who keeps distractions away.

Every now and then, when she is outside, Frieda makes a lunge toward one of the barn cats, but she never goes far or fast, never gets too close, and they no longer pay much attention. Mostly, this is for old times' sake, the glory days when Frieda chased the barn cats up trees and through the pasture. The cats know when to run and when not to. They no longer run from Frieda.

Her days of chasing chipmunks and rabbits are gone. She hasn't taken off into the woods or broken out of the yard in months, and she spends more time now sleeping on her many comfortable dog beds, lying by Maria when she reads or does one of her puzzles. Frieda owns the carpet in front of the wood-stove. No other dog goes near it.

The other day a chipmunk came right up onto the porch where Frieda was napping. Even just a few months ago, that would have provoked a wild and murderous charge. But this time, Frieda stared at the bold little thing for the longest while, and the chipmunk stared back. And then, just like that, the chipmunk was gone and Frieda went back to sleep.

Other things have changed. Rose and Izzy both died in 2011, and Frieda's position in the house and in the pack seems more clear, more secure. Rose was also a dominant female, and she and Frieda often growled and glowered at each other. The other dogs—my new dog, Red, a border collie from Ireland, and Lenore—do not challenge Frieda in any way. She is the undisputed queen of Bedlam Farm. She is royalty: wise, aging, with a storied and wonderful past. She is treated with respect, and has earned her comfort and dignity.

So Frieda and I are in our autumn together. My love and admiration for this very spectacular creature has only grown. Her great heart. Her bravery. Her devotion. She and I were both given a second chance, and both of us took it and ran with it.

And if I do say so, I think she's pretty sweet on me. She can be a downright cuddlebug. She not only lets me touch her, she demands belly scratches, hugs, nuzzling. She is a flirt. Some-times when I wake up in the middle of the night, as I tend to do, worrying about one thing or another, she comes up off her dog bed, next to our bed, and puts her great head in my hand or alongside the mattress. I scratch the side of her nose, which she loves, and she sighs and grumbles some more—her way of saying she loves me, I think.

When I come into the house, she rushes up to me and presses her head against my leg. Those wintry days in the barn now seem a very long way off.

The love story deepens and matures, like a good wine. A happy ending.

The love story is not just me and Frieda. It's Frieda and Maria, and me and Maria, too.

The best fairy tales, I think, happen when animals help bring love to people. There is something magical, almost beyond imagination, when a love exceeds expectations. Love is supposed to fade for those growing older.

That has not happened. The joy of my life is Maria, and the joy of that love is seeing her blossom and grow, morph like a caterpillar to a butterfly before my eyes. We both needed to grow up, take control of our lives. She is doing that, every day.

And then, of course, there is love itself, the point. For a long time, I feared that I was too old to love Maria properly, but it is my turn to cry when she tells me how loved she feels. I am always working to love her—so far, so good. And I will keep at it, to the end, for loving Maria is the best job I have ever had or will have.

We support each other always, but we have also learned to laugh at ourselves and the panics and fears we have carried through life.

For the truth is, she is stronger than me now in many ways, and clearer. I am happy for her, proud of her, rooting for her, always. I am happy to do my work and make way for the gift of her, and her growing presence and skill. She is at her peak now, and I am peeking over the other side of mine.

What a miracle. What a wonderful place to be.

The poet Rumi says to gamble everything for love if you're a true human being. We did. We are.

A Note to the Reader

If you would like to meet Frieda, we have a video for
you online: bedlamfarm.com/meet-frieda

Maria's website is www.fullmoonfiberart.com

Acknowledgments

Thanks to Jen Smith, Andy Barzvi, Christopher Schelling, and Rosemary Ahern for the thought and care that went into this book. And to the workers at the Queensbury, New York, ASPCA who figured out how to capture Frieda after many attempts and get her into the shelter and into a new home. Thanks to the people who knew Frieda in South Glens Falls, who wish to remain anonymous. They were a great help to me. I want to give special thanks to Hannah Elnan, who worked so hard and skillfully on the editing of this book. I am also grateful to my dogs for accepting Frieda into our home and for not getting eaten. I guess there are times when you have to quit on a dog, but I'm glad I didn't quit on Frieda.

About the Author

JON KATZ has written twenty-five books, including works of nonfiction, novels, short stories, and books for children; he is also a photographer. He has written for *The New York Times, The Wall Street Journal,* Slate, *Rolling Stone,* and the *AKC Gazette* and has worked for CBS News, *The Boston Globe, The Washington Post,* and *The Philadelphia Inquirer.* He lives on Bedlam Farm, in upstate New York, with his wife, the artist Maria Wulf, and their dogs, donkeys, barn cats, sheep, and chickens.

About the Type

This book was set in Garamond, a typeface originally designed by the Parisian type cutter Claude Garamond (1480–1561). This version of Garamond was modeled on a 1592 specimen sheet from the Egenolff-Berner foundry, which was produced from types assumed to have been brought to Frankfurt by the punch cutter Jacques Sabon (d. 1580).

Claude Garamond's distinguished romans and italics first appeared in *Opera Ciceronis* in 1543–44. The Garamond types are clear, open, and elegant.